Managing Security in Outsourced and Offshored Environments

Managing Security in Outsourced and Offshored Environments

How to safeguard intellectual assets in a virtual business world

David Lacey

First published in the UK in 2010
by
BSI
389 Chiswick High Road
London W4 4AL

Typeset in Frutiger by Helius – www.helius.biz
Printed in Great Britain by Berforts Group. www.berforts.com

British Library Cataloguing in Publication Data
A catalogue record for this book is available from the British Library

ISBN 978 0 580 68701 3

Contents

Contents

Contents

David is one of the rare breed of security professionals, possessing an encyclopaedic breadth of knowledge about security while, at the same time, having a depth of understanding that you know has been won from long and hard experience. What really makes David stand out is that he always has an interesting point of view, often with a fresh perspective on the challenges of security, and is clear about what needs to be done. He is also well respected for expressing his views, and can do so in a clear and concise way as a blogger, an author, a presenter, or even as a consultant.

Dr Alastair MacWillson
Global Managing Director, Accenture Technology Consulting

Outsourcing key business services or moving to cloud computing is not without risk but can be managed. David Lacey has drawn upon 20 years' experience and a significant industry study to write the handbook every manager should read before they sign the contract.

Professor Paul Dorey
Visiting Professor, Royal Holloway, University of London

Acknowledgements

This book could not have been written without the advice and insights of experts and colleagues from many different fields: outsourcing consultants, lawyers, procurement managers, programme directors and information security specialists. I am especially grateful for the advice and contributions of my professional security colleagues, including Jericho Forum luminaries Paul Dorey, Nick Bleech and Andrew Yeomans, who contributed valuable perspectives on outsourcing and cloud computing from a large customer perspective.

I'd also like to thank my expert legal friends Clare Wardle and Dai Davies, who have unparalleled experience in translating business security aspirations into commercial agreements. Further thanks go to Jim Reed and David Craig, my former colleagues at the Royal Mail Group, for teaching me many of the 'tricks of the trade' for achieving successful large-scale procurement and outsourcing.

I am grateful also to the UK Government's Cyber Security Knowledge Transfer Network for allowing me to draw on previous research on this subject, as well as the Jericho Forum for allowing me to include their ideas on the different models of 'cloud computing' service delivery and use.

Special mentions also go to Philip Virgo, Secretary General of the Information Society Alliance EURIM, for contributing some gems of wisdom on outsourcing and offshoring, Nick Bleech (again) and Dick Price for reviewing the manuscript, and to Dr Alastair MacWillson of Accenture for contributing an enthusiastic, insightful forward.

Finally, special thanks go to Julia Helmsley of BSI, without whose constant enthusiasm, encouragement and support I could not have completed this book.

David Lacey

Foreword

I have known David for over 15 years now and bump into him from time to time, mostly at security conferences, where he is to be seen absorbing key messages and casting an analytical and sometimes critical eye over the issues of the day, the opinions, and the proffered 'solutions' that are often promoted. David is one of the rare breed of security professionals, possessing an encyclopaedic breadth of knowledge about security while, at the same time, having a depth of understanding that you know has been won from long and hard experience. What really makes David stand out is that he always has an interesting point of view, often with a fresh perspective on the challenges of security, and is clear about what needs to be done. He is also well respected for expressing his views, and can do so in a clear and concise way as a blogger, an author, a presenter, or even as a consultant.

It was in that context, at a conference in London, that I met with David last. As we do when we meet, we shared experiences of things we'd seen or done in the security space, hitting on aspects of security that were topical, hot, or even controversial. At that meeting we talked about the security challenges presented by the move to 'cloud'-based services, and how they differed to those challenges that organizations already have to deal with when they outsource or offshore aspects of their business IT systems and processes. David mentioned to me that he was finishing a book on managing security in outsourced and offshored environments, and asked me if I would be willing to write a foreword for the book. This is my attempt to do the subject, and David, justice.

If you are an IT or security professional, you would have to have been hiding for the past five years not to notice the inexorable move towards outsourcing and offshoring initiatives by most major organizations. While these ideas are certainly not new, until now the alternative sourcing of IT has generally been the preserve of the big corporations and organizations, where the maturity and benefits of such services, in terms of costs, performance and flexibility, are assumed to be understood and proven in practice. They are considered a common rather than an extraordinary feature of IT procurement across the Global 5000.

However, over the past couple of years there has been a noticeable growth of interest in third-party services from a wider variety of business and

---

organizations, in more and more geographies, and at all scales on the size spectrum. Why is this? There is no doubt that the economic recession has heaped further pressure on most organizations to do more at much lower cost, which is what the third-party IT sourcing model promises to deliver. In many cases, the business models for the use of such services have been proven, and the returns and benefits of cost reduction, flexibility, performance and usability demonstrated. But I think the real fuel powering this change, and the reason some think we have reached a tipping point on third-party services, is technology innovation in areas that enable new business models around the provision of infrastructure, platforms and applications. Innovations such as virtualization, improving open standards, the development of identity management and better cryptography, to name a few, have all come together to make outsourcing, offshoring and, 'as-a-service' multi-tenancy models more accessible, more acceptable and more desirable for many.

This brings me to the main theme of the book: 'how to safeguard intellectual assets in a virtual business world'. While I have described the growing rush towards alternative sourcing of IT services, I haven't mentioned the risks (old and some new) posed by these new IT models, and the security measures needed to combat them. I'm going to do the sensible thing and leave most of that to David. I would say, however, that the risks and security requirements for such services have usually been thought through, and that there are tried and tested solutions available. But, just looking at press reports of breaches in recent months, I should add that this is not always the case!

What increases the security challenge for many organizations is that they are operating within an increasingly complex and fast-moving business landscape, with growing security threats to worry about, while wrestling with an ever-expanding flood of regulatory compliance demands. New business models and increasingly sophisticated and globally interconnected business processes have outpaced not only regulations designed to ensure security and data protection, but also many organizations' own ability to effectively secure sensitive data. All this requires management to give much closer attention to managing the risks to sensitive data and protecting key information services than they have in the past. Who said the CISO's job is easy …

On a closing note to this introduction, I should declare that I am a great advocate of outsourcing, offshoring and the new 'cloud'-based, 'as-a-service' models of service provision, when it makes business sense, where the risks are fully understood or dealt with and when it is done well! However, organizations considering this direction should collaborate only with business partners that take equal or greater care with data, and rigorously assess partners' knowledge, practices and experience in managing sensitive data across organizational and national boundaries, and in accordance with local privacy laws and industry regulations. Organizations must be vigilant when it comes to confirming the security posture of the companies with which they do business, especially as business takes them to countries with differing standards for data protection and privacy. Always remember the maxim: *choose your business partners with care!*

Dr Alastair MacWillson
Global Managing Director Security Practice, Accenture

1 Introduction

1.1 Purpose

Outsourcing and offshoring of IT services and business processes are powerful business improvement practices, which are capable of delivering impressive cost savings and operational benefits. At the same time, they introduce many significant changes to the supply chain. In particular, they bring about a major transformation of business, technology and security risk profiles. With growing concerns about fraud and espionage set against a background of increasing regulatory compliance demands to safeguard personal data, the implications for security and privacy have become one of the most significant issues for any organization planning a major outsourcing or offshoring initiative. There is surprisingly little published guidance, however, on how to go about specifying and managing the security issues associated with outsourcing and offshoring. This book aims to fill that gap by setting out practical advice, methods and best practices for identifying and managing the security risks associated with the outsourcing and offshoring of IT or business services.

1.2 Audience

The contents of this book will naturally be of interest to information security managers involved in outsourcing or offshoring initiatives. But the book is also aimed at a wider audience of general business managers, CIOs, risk managers, auditors, legal advisers, procurement managers, management consultants, as well as university students studying IT, information security or business studies. Even small-to-medium enterprises will find this book of use when considering the benefits of outsourcing or offshoring services. No prior knowledge or qualifications are required to understand the general points and principles of the book, though many of the checklists include some specialist terminology.

1.3 Scope

Safeguarding intellectual assets in a virtual business world is the major theme of the book, but this book is much broader than security. It also contains many lessons for successful IT governance, procurement and operational excellence, as well as for general business risk mitigation. The book is also much more than

---

just a useful set of security checklists and references, as might be found in a security standard, guideline or code of practice on the subject. In particular, it aims to address not only the numerous security risks and requirements associated with outsourcing, but also the crucial 'softer' management issues, such as how to go about managing the inevitable politics, negotiations and relationship issues associated with virtual partnerships. These softer issues are generally the key factors that will ultimately determine the success or failure of an outsourcing programme.

1.4 Limitations

A word of warning: this book is neither a complete security manual, nor a comprehensive commercial guide to outsourcing. There is much more to these extensive subject areas than can be accommodated in a single book of this size. The scope of this book is strictly confined to the security management issues associated with outsourcing and offshoring. As such, it covers a broad range of topics, including relevant security, commercial and human resources issues.

This book aims to provide many useful insights, tips and warnings about legal and procurement considerations and problems. It is anticipated, however, that any organization setting out to outsource business services would be well supported by professional legal and commercial advisers. In practice, most of the routine, detailed contractual aspects of the contract will be comfortably dealt with by the organization's legal and commercial functions.

The book therefore focuses primarily on the *practical* and *specialist* security management issues associated with outsourcing and offshoring. It is not intended to be a detailed, prescriptive handbook on how to go about outsourcing a set of services or processes.

1.5 Provenance

You might be wondering about the reliability and provenance of the advice contained in this book, especially as this is a subject area demanding both security and outsourcing experience, a combination of knowledge that is rare to encounter in practice. In fact, it is based largely on my own experiences as a senior security and technology director, including two decades of practical experience in specifying and managing the security, governance and risk management requirements for large commercial contracts, including a few in excess of a billion pounds in value.

I have aimed to augment my own personal perspective with advice gathered through interviews and workshops with other experienced practitioners from a variety of fields including IT management, security, risk management, human resources, internal audit, procurement and legal services. The book also builds on an earlier research project carried out on this subject, sponsored by the UK Government Cyber Security Knowledge Transfer Network, to whom I am grateful for their kind permission to include some of the findings of that study.

1.6 Content and structure

The material in this book is designed to be accessible to business, IT and security managers with no specialist technical or security knowledge. The contents are structured in a logical sequence, reflecting the lifecycle of outsourcing: from conception through definition, selection, negotiation, implementation and management until the eventual termination of the outsourced services.

Chapter 2 explains some of the fundamental principles and concepts behind outsourcing.

Chapter 3 explores various types of outsourcing arrangement and the risks they introduce.

Chapter 4 examines the business drivers for outsourcing and their impact on security.

Chapter 5 considers the key areas of planning and preparation required prior to outsourcing.

Chapter 6 examines the security considerations associated with selecting an outsourcing supplier.

Chapter 7 looks at the security issues and requirements for developing and negotiating the outsourcing contract and supporting schedules

Chapter 8 discusses the considerations and activities involved in implementing a new outsourcing arrangement

---

Chapter 9 covers the issues and considerations involved in successfully managing the outsourcing relationship

Chapter 10 examines the planning considerations and issues concerned with the eventual termination of the contract.

Chapter 11 explores the security issues associated with the adoption of Internet-based 'cloud computing' services

Each chapter also contains a useful summary of key learning points. For the impatient among you, this might be a useful starting point to grasp the salient issues.

2 Fundamentals of outsourcing

2.1 The case for and against outsourcing

2.1.1 The hazards of change

'Better the devil you know than the devil you don't' is an old proverb which means that it's generally better to deal with someone or something you are familiar with, even if you don't like them, rather than take a risk with an unknown person or thing which could turn out to be worse. Regardless of the fact that IT managers are not the most popular company staff, it's clear that contemporary business has consciously decided to ignore this 16th-Century pearl of wisdom.

Outsourcing and offshoring of IT services and business processes are expanding management practices, attracting impressive, double-digit annual growth. Today's outsourcing industry is mature and competitive. It is an established practice, not just a management fad. Organizations across all sectors are embracing outsourcing and offshoring, despite the fact that many enterprises have found that, in practice, the cost and complexity associated of outsourcing services is not quite as simple as they might have originally anticipated.

Why should outsourcing and offshoring be so popular? Any major change in the sourcing of IT services is bound to be disruptive, involve unpopular decisions and demand a good deal of advance planning, significant up-front expense, and substantial procurement effort, often for little or no visible improvement in the services that are to be delivered. Executive boards often complain of service quality and organizational culture, but achieving a major change is always difficult and often hazardous.

As the Italian philosopher, Machiavelli famously put it:

> It must be considered that there is nothing more difficult to carry out, nor more doubtful of success, nor more dangerous to handle, than to initiate a new order of things. For the reformer has enemies in all those who profit by the old order, and only lukewarm defenders in all those who would profit by the new order, this reticence arising partly from fear of their adversaries, who have the laws in their favour; and partly from the incredulity of mankind, who do not truly believe in anything new until they have had actual

experience of it. Thus it arises that on every opportunity for attacking the reformer, his opponents do so with the zeal of partisans, the others only defend him half-heartedly, so that between them he runs great danger.[1]

In the case of outsourcing, the change agent is rarely intimidated by such threats, as this agent is often – though not always – the management team, supported by the executive board and an outside team of advisers. But the hazards remain. Outsourcing is a high-risk initiative, with a mixed track record that includes many examples of expensive failures. Looked at from that perspective, it raises the obvious question of why outsourcing should be such an attractive management practice. In fact, the answer is quite simple. The benefits are simply irresistible.

2.1.2 Irresistible benefits

There are three highly persuasive factors that are guaranteed to compel most managing directors to seek to externalize the source of their supplies and services.

The first persuasive factor is that externalizing any internal service opens up an opportunity for short-term savings and a potential injection of cash through the sale of the associated assets. Such returns are always welcome to hard-pressed business directors. Guaranteed cash today is always more attractive than projected savings tomorrow.

The second factor is that outsourcing transforms a fixed set of costs into a variable on-demand payment. And that is essential for any organization that's planning to slim down, freeze investment, cut operating costs or reduce headcount, especially when facing a recession. Many directors will commit to a higher rental rate in future years, if it enables immediate cost reductions to meet business targets this financial year.

The third factor is that the outcome of outsourcing is an apparent increase in the revenue generated per individual employee, which is an attractive target for many senior executives. Shareholders and investors pay close attention to such ratios. It's the type of outcome that chief executive officers like to achieve in order to bolster their personal reputation and market value.

---

[1] Niccolo Machiavelli, *The Prince* (1532)

There are, of course, other important business factors that make outsourcing attractive, but they are generally the arguments that are used to *justify* the action of outsourcing, rather than to *compel* directors to take it. Typical examples might be the possibility of achieving an injection of new skills, or perhaps establishing a new global support capability. But these goals are the icing on the cake rather than the primary drivers.

2.1.3 The downside of outsourcing

There are also many risks associated with outsourcing, both commercial and security risks, and these are progressively increasing with the growing ambition, complexity and size of modern outsourcing contracts, coupled with the increasing loss of visibility and direct control over day-to-day operations as sources of supply become more remote and anonymous.

A further negative factor is the inevitable commercial reality that a significant profit margin will need to be extracted by the outsourcer in order to justify taking on the task. This is a guaranteed overhead that must be taken into account in any business case for outsourcing, unless the customer believes that they are smart enough to haggle a cost-price deal with an outsourcer, which can be a dangerous tactic from a quality of service perspective.

The simple fact, however, is that despite all the risks, the overheads, the extra effort and the potential longer-term penalties, outsourcing continues to be an attractive option to executive boards. And that is because the benefits mentioned above are more compelling than the risks.

Outsourcing and offshoring are double-edged swords. Managed well, they represent a smart business strategy that delivers major benefits, such as reduced costs, easier scalability of services or access to a broader pool of specialist skills and resources. Managed badly, they become an inflexible, expensive millstone that restricts future innovation and growth. Without adequate planning and prudent management controls, outsourcing and offshoring can introduce unacceptable levels of new risks, such as the possibility of a breach of confidential data or a sustained outage of essential services.

These risks will need to be contained through proactive governance and controls. In fact, the critical success factors for both effective service delivery and prudent security management are the same. Success in both areas requires careful planning and preparation; good understanding and management of risks;

professional specification of services; prudent negotiation of the contract; close alignment of objectives with the supplier; and continuous, proactive relationship management.

2.2 What's special about outsourcing?

2.2.1 More than just a division of labour

Outsourcing and offshoring of business services might be contemporary and relatively modern management trends, but there is nothing new about the concept of externalizing the source of supplies and services. The process of contracting out work is a longstanding one. In fact, it's a natural form of the long-established principle of 'division of labour'. For centuries, enterprises have elected to farm out selected activities to specialist outside companies or individuals who are able to deliver a better product or service at a lower cost.

What's different about outsourcing and offshoring programmes, compared to traditional contracting out, is that these initiatives represent a step change in the approach to the transfer of in-house work to an outside agency, generally on a much larger scale and for a much longer period of time. In terms of management complexity and organizational disruption, there is simply no comparison between the employment of an external supplier of raw materials to the outsourcing of a critical business process or a portfolio of computer applications. The procurement process is longer and more complex, the returns and risks are substantially higher, and the consequences are likely to have a significant impact at a higher level in the business value chain.

Outsourcing of IT services is also very different from the externalization of well-understood, 'commodity' business services such as accounting or legal services. Each situation is different of course, but a typical portfolio of information systems within a medium or large organization is likely to contain many bespoke elements that will require careful consideration, meticulous specification and supervised migration. In many cases this will demand a substantial in-house planning effort, lasting perhaps one or even two years. Such a programme should not be undertaken lightly, nor without due consideration of the full, longer-term implications and the eventual longer-term exit strategy.

Offshoring introduces the additional risk of a transfer of work to a different country, enabling a potentially greater cost saving, but also presenting a new set of management challenges. In fact, the limited experience of many organizations in managing such arrangements suggests there is still a good deal of uncertainty about what constitutes best practice in mitigating these risks. A further factor is that what looks like a good deal today might not appear so in future years. Changes in labour costs, exchange rates and regulatory compliance requirements, for example, are continuing to transform the cost–benefit equation as well as the risk profile associated with such initiatives.

2.2.2 A growing management challenge

The size of the challenge is also steadily increasing. For the past two decades, the scope of outsourcing and offshoring programmes has become progressively deeper and more radical, as both service providers and customer organizations are tempted to stretch the boundaries of outsourcing arrangements: from selected individual services to entire business processes; and from local delivery of dedicated services to the global provision of virtual services, shared with many other clients.

Emerging technology is also accelerating the move of business applications from secure servers sited within private data centres, towards Internet-based services operating across a virtual 'cloud' of shared, networked infrastructure. These trends are changing the nature of the financial benefits and the operational risks, as well as introducing challenging new security, compliance and business exposures.

The world of outsourcing and offshoring is characterized by a constantly changing landscape. We continue to encounter new terms describing emerging variants or fashions in outsourcing and offshoring: 'multi-sourcing' to describe the provision of outside services from a range of different suppliers, or 'near-shoring' to suggest the delivery of services from a country nearer to home, or at least nearer in culture. The decision, for example, by German car manufacturer BMW in 2008 to extend its manufacturing operations in North America made many observers think again about the validity of traditional assumptions about the economics of offshoring.

The major implication for security practitioners, either in-house or external, is that they must all raise their game. Senior decision makers need incisive input on the risks and consequences of outsourcing decisions. Outsourcing demands the resolution of complex interrelated problems across multidisciplinary virtual teams. It requires considerable, detailed work to understand the many security issues and to overcome them.

The skills involved in conducting due diligence and management of external relationships demand a broader perspective than that required to perform traditional security reviews and compliance audits, especially when dealing with unfamiliar social or political cultures.

2.3 What changes when we outsource?

2.3.1 Unavoidable changes

Outsourcing and offshoring offer substantial business benefits, but they also introduce a number of new security risks. These risks cannot be avoided and must therefore be accepted or mitigated in some way. The most significant of these risks arise from the following fundamental changes to the services that are outsourced:

- a major loss in visibility of operating practices, risks and events and incidents associated with the delivery of the outsourced services;
- the removal of direct control over the development, operation and maintenance of outsourced services and products;
- a substantial reduction in communication with and access to the staff delivering the services;
- changes in security responsibilities, affecting both customer and outsourcer;
- changes in IT and business governance processes, including compliance, risk management, business continuity and internal and external audit, on both sides of the partnership;
- a shift in loyalties, from the customer to the service provider, for the staff tasked to deliver the services;
- a potential change in the location of services and data, which might have an impact on the legal environment;
- strictly limited access to facilities and staff to perform audits, reviews or security investigations.

Later paragraphs in this chapter examine some of these changes in more detail.

2.3.2 Responsibilities that do not change

Despite the transfer of control of day-to-day service delivery, ultimate responsibility for security, privacy, compliance, and the consequences of risks relating to the outsourced services and information will remain firmly with the customer. It is simply not acceptable to leave all decisions on security to the outsourcer. The customer has an obligation to ensure that legal and regulatory compliance requirements will continue to be met from the outset, and that the interests of shareholders, business partners, customers and staff are adequately safeguarded under the new arrangements.

The customer must anticipate and plan for the changes in security responsibilities that will occur when a service is outsourced. Although many responsibilities remain the same, the way they are executed will change considerably. In particular, the customer must identify, specify and oversee many security requirements. In practice, this will require the development and maintenance of a new layer of formal documentation, as well as the design and operation of a new set of management processes.

2.3.3 New loyalties

Responsiveness and eagerness by a contractor to meet short-term commercial requirements should not be confused with a commitment to serve the longer-term interests of the organization. Contractors are servants of business, and might appear keen to go the extra mile, but they will never match the motivation of in-house employees.

It might sound cynical, but it's worth taking note of Machiavelli's shrewd observations on outside agencies:

> *Mercenary and auxiliary forces are useless and dangerous; and if one holds his state based on these arms, he will stand neither firm nor safe; for they are disunited, ambitious, and without discipline, unfaithful, valiant before friends, cowardly before enemies; they have neither the fear of God nor fidelity to men, and destruction is deferred only so long as the attack is; for in peace one is robbed by them, and in war by the enemy. The fact is, they have no other attraction or reason for keeping the field than a trifle of stipend, which is not sufficient to make them willing to die for you. They are ready enough to be your soldiers whilst you do not make war, but if war comes they take themselves off or run from the foe.[2]*

---

[2] Mercenary forces are troops hired to fight for a wage. Auxiliary forces are troops borrowed from an ally. Machievalli believed that auxiliary forces are more dangerous because they are united under their own interests and controlled by capable leaders who may turn against their employers.

Such a perspective might seem unduly pessimistic perhaps, but it underlines the importance of recognising the fact that loyalties will be markedly different following an outsourcing initiative.

2.3.4 Loss of visibility and communications

Managing security is always more difficult across an external partnership. Visibility and control of threats, vulnerabilities and events lie at the heart of effective security and risk management. If you can't see what's happening on the ground, then you can't really determine what to do, or when and how to intervene. At the same time, the service provider lacks visibility of business developments at the customer end that might shape the nature or significance of a security risk or its impact.

Organizations considering how best to manage business processes that extend across a virtual supply chain should heed the advice of the late W. Edwards Deming, the renowned author and management consultant, who included in his seven deadly sins of management (that plague Western business) the sin of: 'running a company on visible figures alone'. Customers should never be content to rely solely on the information that is routinely provided by the outsourcer. Prudent managers need to identify the information they will need to manage the partnership, and make appropriate arrangements to obtain it.

Any externalization of services inevitably places greater distance of user management from the staff taking day-to-day operational decisions, and the circumstances surrounding their analysis. Understanding the context of a decision or event is important to fully appreciate its significance. A little knowledge can be a catalyst to jump to a misleading conclusion.

Statistics can easily be misinterpreted when taken out of context. 'Chinese whispers' and hearsay are also rife across business partnerships, especially those where there is tension arising from differences in interpretation of requirements or unresolved disputes. Assumptions based on incomplete information should be avoided. Facts need to be gathered and assessed in an objective way, within a defined, well-understood context. New systems will be necessary to enable this.

2.4 The implications for information and security governance

2.4.1 The need for new structures

Given sufficient resources and budget, most risks associated with outsourcing and offshoring can either be prevented or contained at an acceptable level. One overriding risk must, however, be accepted with open eyes: there will be an inevitable, immediate loss of visibility and direct control of activities and events, yet accountability for the impact of security breaches will remain firmly with the customer organization.

Risk profiles are also likely to change considerably over time, with changes in the business, legal and security landscapes. New governance structures must therefore be developed to extend management oversight across the new supply chain. Suppliers must be willing and able to support these new arrangements.

The major challenge is to establish an effective means to ensure that the day-to-day management of security remains in step with the evolving requirements of the business. This requires, among other things, a number of key conditions to be met:

- appropriate confirmation that the service provider remains willing and capable of meeting the customer's level of security;
- a contract specifying a minimum level of controls that meets the customer's security requirements;
- a formal process for specifying and agreeing changes in customer security requirements;
- a process for reporting changes in services that might impact the customer;
- a governance process that can operate effectively across the partnership;
- an assurance process to confirm that the service provider is continuing to manage security, as specified and required.

Achieving these goals is not trivial. It demands careful planning and attention to detail in specifying requirements, as well as sound governance of the services actually delivered. If this sounds more like advice on management rather than security, it's because good security and risk management are primarily achieved through sound management. They are, in fact, two sides of the same coin.

2.4.2 The impact on risk management and business continuity

New processes will need to be established to ensure security and business continuity, to manage security and business risks, and to demonstrate continuing regulatory compliance and data protection requirements. It should never be assumed that the supplier will automatically establish and address the risk profile and compliance requirements of the business customers without the input, demands and agreement of the user organization.

Existing risk management, business continuity and crisis management processes will need to be significantly revised to operate across the supply chain. This will mean, among other things, harmonising standards, structures and procedures for assessing and addressing risks, as well as for identifying, investigating and responding to security incidents.

The overall risk profile, post-outsourcing, might in fact be very different. In particular, there might well be greater scope for data security breaches. But there will certainly be new, longer-term business and security risks, including the impact of becoming locked into a particular supplier or product, which could result in significantly higher charges, new security exposures, reduced options for business continuity plans and a potential loss of business agility.

No organization should proceed with a major outsourcing or offshoring commitment without careful consideration of the full range of associated security risks. The budget for developing and implementing new processes and new business and security controls should be factored into the projected costs of the proposed outsourcing arrangement.

Small companies, in particular, should consider how much they can actually afford to lose from a failed arrangement. In serious cases, such failures might lead to a major loss in cash flow, which could result in bankruptcy. Larger companies might be better equipped to ride out short-term losses, reflecting the fact that what might constitute an acceptable risk for a large organization could well prove to be fatal for a smaller one.

Small and medium-sized enterprises are also less likely to have the experience and skills on hand to identify and assess the wide range of security risks associated with a major change in service provision. Where possible, therefore, smaller companies should seek specialist external information security advice. For a small company, a small up-front cost for consultants or lawyers might be highly unattractive. But it will prove to be an acceptable charge if it helps avoid substantially larger, longer-term penalties or, in the worst case, a damaging incident or situation that results in bankruptcy.

2.4.3 The changing compliance landscape

Outsourcing is generally a long-term arrangement, though there is a current trend towards shorter contracts. Organizations must think beyond today's security threats and compliance requirements and anticipate what new risks or regulatory requirements might emerge during the lifetime of the arrangement.

We cannot predict the future precisely, but one trend is very clear at present, and that is that security and compliance demands are steadily growing, and the impact of data breaches is becoming increasingly serious. It is sensible, therefore, to anticipate a tighter future security and regulatory regime, and ensure that policies and standards can be extended or raised when required.

One of the major shifts in the business landscape has been the slow but seemingly inevitable rise in the power, scope and demands of regulators and, in particular, the global growth in legal and regulatory requirements to safeguard personal data and notify regulators and customers of data breaches. This trend seems set to continue.

Stewart Room,[3] a partner in the law firm Field Fisher Waterhouse, describes this trend of growing compliance expectations as a 'bear market', fuelled by a tendency for politicians and regulators to respond to reported data breaches with ever tougher demands.

The characteristics of a bear market are a loss in confidence, a negative sentiment and a growing pessimism about the likelihood of organizations delivering on their commitments. This certainly applies to data security and privacy. It's no exaggeration to suggest that even regulators have lost confidence in their own ability to prevent major data breaches. When such a situation is reached, there is likely to be a trend towards more disputes and litigation, and a progression from data protection being an implied legal requirement to that of an express requirement.

---

[3] Stewart Room is the author of *Butterworth's Data Security Law & Practice*.

Political interests shape emerging laws and politicians understand that consumer-friendly initiatives are potential vote winners. Strong security governance creates a better impression with citizens and tough legislation is easy to implement at little cost to the government purse. Such considerations might help explain why Governor of California Arnold Schwarzenegger was minded to introduce a data breach notification law in 2003, an idea which has subsequently been adopted and extended, with enthusiasm, by other politicians and regulators across the world.

This trend suggests that user organizations should make tougher security demands over the services delivered by outsourcers than might have previously been accepted in earlier contracts. In the past, many smaller organizations were happy to adopt the terms, conditions and security posture of an outsourcer with few questions asked and little direct consequence. That will not do for the future. Regulators and customers will expect a higher degree of due diligence, strict contractual demands, and a capability to monitor day-to-day operations and events. Otherwise, directors might eventually find themselves vulnerable to steep fines, jail sentences and the prospect of class actions by customers.

2.5 Key requirements for success

2.5.1 The 'Golden Triangle'

Regardless of the specific security and regulatory requirements, successful management of any outsourcing arrangement will always demand close attention by all parties, both customer and supplier, to three fundamental, underpinning requirements:

1) a good contract that is comprehensive and unambiguous, yet sufficiently flexible to accommodate future change;
2) a healthy relationship that is built on shared incentives, good diplomacy and efficient communications;
3) a sound set of management processes that are fully understood, accepted and adhered to by both parties.

These three key requirements can be thought of as the interconnected points of a 'Golden Triangle': a management model that represents both the problem space associated with outsourcing and offshoring, as well as the potential solution space for addressing these risks and issues. Figure 1 illustrates the interaction and relationships between these factors.

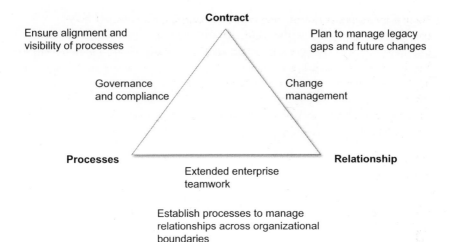

Contract

Ensure alignment and
visibility of processes

Plan to manage legacy
gaps and future changes

Governance
and compliance

Change
management

Processes

Relationship

Extended enterprise
teamwork

Establish processes to manage
relationships across organizational
boundaries

**Figure 1 – The 'Golden Triangle': Key requirements for successful
management of outsourcing programmes**

2.5.2 Vehicles for achieving success

Figure 1 highlights three important vehicles for the successful security
management of any outsourcing or offshoring programme:

1) attention to governance and compliance, especially the alignment and
   visibility of management processes;
2) good management of change, including the agreed approach to manage
   legacy gaps between current requirements and the actual delivery of services,
   as well as a capability to address future changes;
3) extended-enterprise teamwork, including the establishment of governance
   processes to manage activities and relationships that span organizational
   boundaries.

In practice, the majority of organizations focus most effort on the challenging
task of getting the paperwork right to support the outsourcing arrangement,
especially the contract schedules and the specification of the services to be
delivered. This is an understandable tendency, sometimes reinforced by the fact
that the project team responsible for planning and managing the outsourcing
programme might not be tasked with the longer-term implementation and
management of the arrangement.

There are countless cases of organizations that have spent dozens of man-years of effort in defining the requirements for outsourcing, confidently anticipating that these will be translated into action with minimal oversight. But the reality is that few operational staff actually read the fine detail of the contract. The delivery of customer services will be primarily based on the outsourcer's existing capabilities, shaped by the contract and also by the demands of the client's governance processes and day-to-day management of relationships.

2.5.3 Getting the balance right

Experience indicates that the real keys to successful service delivery are a good working relationship and a set of well-aligned management processes. But all of the factors mentioned are interdependent. A bad contract, for example, will encourage a bad relationship. And that in turn will reduce the quality of services delivered.

Remedying such a difficult situation requires close attention to the needs and behaviour of the people on both sides of the partnership. It's easier to mend a broken relationship or design a better governance structure than it is to change a bad contract. And, given time, a good working relationship supported by a good set of management processes can help to overcome the constraints of a bad contract.

Successful service delivery and security both depend ultimately on a sound contract, good cross-organizational teamwork, and a set of interfaces and processes that are practical and acceptable to all players. Clearly, it's better to get all of these things right from the outset. But it should also be remembered that when things have gone wrong it's never too late to introduce good working practices into an established partnership.

Every outsourcing or offshoring programme is different. Each situation presents a unique blend of management challenges, regulatory demands and security risks. It's also a fast-changing and evolving field where traditional assumptions might not always apply to emerging issues. Past experience is not necessarily a reliable basis for smart decision-making. What has been known to work in previous contracts is a good starting point, but no organization should proceed without first establishing the associated risks, the current compliance requirements and the longer-term business implications.

2.6 Learning points from this chapter

This chapter has explored the fundamental principles of outsourcing and offshoring. Key learning points to note can be summarized as follows.

▶ Outsourcing and offshoring are growing management practices. There are many associated costs and risks, but the benefits to senior management are irresistible. Key benefits include short-term savings, a variable cost basis and a perceived increase in revenue per employee.

▶ Outsourcing is different from traditional contracting out of business services, because of the greater scale, complexity and organizational disruption. Offshoring introduces additional risks through the change in environment, culture and communications. The economics and risks associated with outsourcing and offshoring are constantly changing, and the level of ambition for organizations to go broader and deeper is progressively growing.

▶ Security risks result from complexity of management, loss of visibility and control, and an inevitable change in loyalty. They need to be contained through proactive governance and controls. Security needs to be addressed at all stages of the outsourcing lifecycle, but early identification of risks is crucial to the business case and the design of the outsourcing programme. New governance systems will also be required to maintain regulatory compliance and stakeholder assurance.

▶ Key requirements for success are: a good contract that is comprehensive, unambiguous, but flexible; a healthy relationship built on shared incentives; good relationship management; and sound management processes that are understood and followed by all parties. Important vehicles for success are: attention to the alignment and visibility of management processes; good management of change; and effective virtual team working across the partnership.

▶ Every outsourcing or offshoring programme is different, presenting a unique set of management challenges, regulatory considerations and security risks. Outsourcing is also a fast-changing field where existing assumptions might not apply to emerging issues. No organization should proceed without first establishing the risks and the longer-term business and compliance implications.

3 Forms of outsourcing and offshoring

3.1 What we mean by outsourcing and offshoring

According to the *Oxford English Dictionary*, outsourcing is obtaining something by contract from an outside supplier. It could be an existing in-house service that's moved outside, or perhaps a new service that's sourced from outside the organization.

There are many variations on this theme. This book will try to cover as many situations as practicable, while aiming to avoid excessive complexity. In general, however, when reference is made to outsourcing, it will be the more challenging task of moving an in-house service to an outside provider that is meant. Many of the security considerations in buying a new service from an outside vendor are similar, though the scope of the problem space is likely to be smaller.

Offshoring adds a further dimension to outsourcing. It describes the relocation by a company of a business process or service from one country to another. This is generally done to reduce costs, though there are other benefits, as we will discuss later in this chapter. Again, it's the externalization of a set of activities but it's a more challenging task as it introduces a new set of risks.

3.2 A global industry

The choice and diversity of outsourcing options is continuously changing and expanding, but there is one clear, underpinning trend. The progressive globalization of both western and eastern outsourcers has created a global industry in which suppliers from both sides of the world can now offer similar services at almost identical rates, delivered to, or from, absolutely anywhere in the world. Location is becoming less important to the supplier, though it still presents major challenges for security, regulatory compliance and due diligence from the customer perspective.

The recent global recession has prompted many organizations to consider outsourcing as a means of achieving a variable cost model for business services that is better able to respond to sudden changes in customer demand or service usage. But outsourcing is far from an easy, instant remedy to falling or rising demands on services. It requires careful planning and prudent management of the increasing number of business and security risks associated with any transfer of custodianship of sensitive data or information services.

These risks cannot be regarded lightly at a time when most organizations face growing regulatory compliance demands and security threats of increasing sophistication. In fact, all indications suggest that both the security risks and the compliance requirements associated with any processing of sensitive information are likely to continue to increase through the lifetime of the outsourcing contract.

3.3 Wide variation in scope

Outsourcing and offshoring are far from standardized processes. Contracts can differ markedly in breadth, depth and granularity, each resulting in a unique set of security problems, risks and cultural challenges. The scope of the outsourcing arrangement can vary considerably:

- it might encompass a business process, an assorted set of IT services, or perhaps an organizational function;
- it might employ a single prime contractor or many individual specialist suppliers (multi-sourcing);
- the contract might be for as little as six months or as long as a decade;
- the services might be sited offshore to deliver services to a local region or simply to save money;
- the applications might be delivered from dedicated computer platforms in a private data centre, or through a virtual infrastructure shared with many other customers;
- the contract might involve a large transfer of staff to the outsourcer, or simply an electronic switch to a new external service.

Regardless of the scope and nature of the contract, it's clear that any significant change to the operating environment of an information system will result in a significant impact on risk profiles, governance arrangements and compliance processes. In some cases, there might also be stringent legal restrictions on what is legally allowed, for example concerning the export or storage of sensitive personal data.

Outsourcing extends beyond information systems, to encompass projects, tasks, organizational functions, and perhaps complete 'end-to-end' business processes. Some activities might remain in-house, but the information supporting the outsourced process will have to operate across a new, changed environment and will be subject to new risks.

3.4 Outsourcing options

Outsourcing and offshoring are just two options within a broad spectrum of choices for externalization of business services. This range of options extends from the simple contracting out of a selection of non-core services, to the establishment of a fully externalized, virtual supply chain. Each choice along this spectrum presents a different set of risks and challenges, but they share many common characteristics; in particular, the need for effective due diligence and for careful consideration and monitoring of the competence, reliability and trustworthiness of the selected suppliers.

This chapter examines various types of external services arrangements and their associated risks and impact, starting with simple contracting out of activities and extending to contemporary models for IT services procurement, such as 'Software as a Service' and 'cloud computing'. In fact, some authorities see outsourcing and cloud computing as early steps on the road to a more ambitious goal of 'everything as a service', a management practice that might describe the supply chain of a complete virtual organization where all services, from product design to marketing, are procured over the Internet from multiple sources.

3.5 Subcontracted services

3.5.1 Third-party security risks

Subcontracting of selected activities and services to a third-party vendor is a widespread, longstanding and, in many cases, essential business activity for all organizations. It enables organizations to design, build, sell and deliver professional products, regardless of the constraints of their in-house skills, resources and manufacturing capability. Any use of third parties to deliver business services, however, introduces risks: these can range from a failure to deliver the required service through incompetence, bankruptcy, or perhaps even as a result of a more sinister act of theft, espionage or sabotage.

In most cases of subcontracting, however, it's unusual to encounter a serious risk from a third-party contractor, as they are generally motivated to continue to win and maintain business from customers. Cases of fraud or failure are bad news for future business. But it should be remembered that many types of security risk and incidents are increasing. And in a fast-changing, competitive marketplace such as IT services, there is likely to be a higher turnover of skilled staff, as well as an increasing pressure to meet short-term business targets, all of which heightens the risks associated with the outsourced delivery of services.

When the pressure is on, checks and supervision can easily slip, and this in turn can attract thieves and fraudsters. No supplier should be assumed to be perfect, regardless of their previous track record.

3.5.2 Growing risks with deeper access

In fact, the risk landscape associated with third-party services is changing quite markedly. In the past, most business and security risks could be satisfactorily mitigated through the use of routine procurement practices such as references, contractual conditions and, if necessary, staff vetting processes. In recent years, however, new dimensions of risk have opened up as third-party contractors have increasingly been allowed deeper and broader access to corporate IT networks and sensitive or critical business databases.

Contractors are now considered by many security experts to be the 'soft underbelly' of large organizations that have valuable, critical or sensitive intellectual assets. And these days, such information is now of interest to a much wider range of external agencies. In practice it's often easier for a hostile party, such as a hostile intelligence service, terrorist group or organized criminal gang to steal or sabotage information from a large organization through its contractors, than it is by means of a direct attack or an infiltration of the customer organization.

The major risk associated with any third-party connection is the fact that many enterprise systems are especially vulnerable to unauthorized access from within the trusted corporate security perimeter. This is because most legacy systems and services were originally designed to deliver services to trusted staff operating within a secure, private physical environment.

Many contractors now bring their own IT support with them, which can range from a laptop PC to remote Internet-based applications. Such facilities can quickly end up processing sensitive customer data using facilities that might not be designed with adequate security in mind. Levels of access to corporate networks and systems granted to contractors can range from the simple act of a visiting contractor connecting a laptop to a corporate network, to the establishment of direct high-speed network connections between enterprise networks.

Even longstanding, contracted-out support functions, such as vehicle fleet management, that have traditionally involved minimal IT content, are now being operated by specialist service providers using sophisticated Internet-based applications. Such systems might be outside of the radar and scope of the in-house security function, but they are likely to contain sensitive information about employees, customers or suppliers. It might be considered a form of 'IT outsourcing by stealth'.

Without clear security policies and standards, responsibility for ensuring the security of contractor access to data can easily fall through the cracks, as customer managers might assume that the security of a contractor's facilities and procedures are outside of their responsibility, and contractors will see no need to upgrade their security practices for an individual client.

3.5.3 Powerful access requires tighter control

The increasing power and capacity of modern client devices also enables contractors with direct network or system access to download large amounts of corporate data onto laptop computers or portable memory devices, few of which are likely to be afforded the same degree of security protection as in-house client devices. We all carry memory sticks around in our pockets, and in practice we rarely treat them with the respect that they deserve. Best intentions alone are never sufficient to safeguard valuable corporate data.

As business cycles become faster and commercial products become more complex, the need for increasingly powerful network access and system privileges for contractors is also likely to grow, increasing the impact of the potential risks presented by the use of third parties. Demands for tighter controls over contractors will be inevitable, as the incidence of major data breaches grows and the regulatory response becomes increasingly tougher.

The range of tasks contracted out to third parties is also growing, as the marketplace for specialist or general service providers matures. In the IT field, one of the most common forms of subcontracting is for system integration activities. This is necessary as few organizations can justify the presence of an in-house pool of specialist skilled staff to support the wide range of systems in a typical applications portfolio, as well as keep up to date with emerging technologies and development methods.

3.5.4 Trusted or trustworthy contractors

In recent years the scope of externally delivered IT services has also grown to encompass security services, including sensitive intrusion detection and incident response processes that require specialist skills but deliver highly confidential outputs, demanding a higher level of trust and confidence in the integrity and behaviour of the staff performing the activities.

Organizations need to make a clear distinction between trustworthy and trusted suppliers. The former label indicates a degree of confidence in the contractor, whereas the latter implies a conscious, or perhaps unconscious, acceptance of the risk arising from a decision to contract out a sensitive service. But regardless of the particular business drivers and considerations the end result is that the customer will have little, if any, control over the selection, supervision and discipline of the staff employed by third-party suppliers.

How far can you trust a contractor that you know nothing about? The answer is that it depends on the experience of the client. Some people are naturally trusting about new people they encounter. Others are highly suspicious. It might be more polite to start by allowing a stranger the initial benefit of the doubt, but I always keep in the back of my mind something I term the 'rule of four'. This rule is based on an assumption that, out of every four people, at least one is likely to have crooked tendencies, another might be honest to the point of naivety, and the remaining two perhaps inclined to take a risk assessment about what they might get away with.

This might not be an entirely fair, accurate or proven assumption, but it's a healthy starting point when managing information security. Many organizations choose to accept the risks from contractors, if for no other reason than the simple fact that they have accepted such risks before without any incident. Clients can aim to mitigate a certain degree of risks through contractual conditions or by demanding a level of security vetting. But there are diminishing returns on the confidence gained from personnel checks, and it is inappropriate to demand security checks that might exceed or fall short of the organization's existing level of security checks for its own recruits.

3.5.5 Legal and compliance considerations

A forward-looking analysis of risks will point to the need for a more controlled approach to subcontracting. Evidence of responsible, appropriate checks in managing contractors is prudent in order to defend against potential accusations of negligence. It would be unconvincing in a court of law, for example, to claim that due diligence, controls and monitoring were unnecessary simply because they had not been found necessary in the past.

Employing non-company staff in a sensitive role will always introduce a degree of risk that needs to be addressed, and seen to be mitigated, either through contractual measures or supervision and monitoring of day-to-day activities and access. The cost of this additional activity needs to be factored into business cases for delegating work beyond the organization's controlled borders.

Regulators are increasingly recognising and drawing attention to the importance of extending security controls across the supply chain. The UK Financial Services Authority warns that, 'Firms have an obligation to look after customer data even when the process has been outsourced to a third party, including mail shot providers and couriers.' The UK Office of Government Commerce has also set mandatory requirements for government contracts involving personal or other confidential information. These requirements include the need for staff vetting as well as controls to safeguard the confidentiality, integrity and availability of the data.

Contractors performing business activities on behalf of the organization must be given a clear statement of their security obligations, including the need to adhere to security policies, standards, classification systems, contractual requirements and relevant legislation and regulatory compliance requirements.

An appropriate business manager should be assigned to 'own' the contractual relationship and ensure that current and future individual contractors understand their obligations, and that the level and method of access to corporate systems and data that is granted is appropriate and terminated when no longer required. A useful approach to managing different levels of access by contractors is to assign trust levels associated with levels of restricted, controlled or supervised access to buildings and systems.

3.6 Outsourced services

3.6.1 A radical form of externalization

Compared to contracting out, outsourcing generally represents a more disruptive transfer of a substantial set of in-house services to an external service provider. When done for the first time, it is likely to require a radical redesign of the function being outsourced, including the division into an in-house contract management function and an outsourced service function. Outsourcing will also significantly affect the size or shape of other supporting in-house functions, such as security, human resources, finance and other administrative services.

From a security perspective, key decisions will be required on which security activities should be outsourced, which should be retained, and which new activities are needed to ensure formal compliance management of the supply chain. These are difficult but important decisions, as they will determine the longer-term capability of the customer organization to successfully govern the security of the outsourced services.

As mentioned earlier, outsourcing also introduces major changes in corporate governance. Failure to anticipate and plan for these changes will undermine the effectiveness and coverage of key corporate processes, such as operational risk management, business continuity planning and regulatory compliance.

3.6.2 Multi-sourcing agreements

Outsourcing arrangements vary greatly in their scope, duration and complexity, each combination presenting a particular, unique set of business and security challenges. From the customer perspective, one of the most significant management decisions is whether to employ a single prime contractor, or several individual specialist suppliers.

The term multi-sourcing is sometimes used to describe large outsourcing agreements that enable a range of different services to be sourced from separate suppliers. In practice, this is a complex, challenging model for customers to manage as it involves a large number of individual relationships. In particular it demands a very clear vision and strategy that sets direction and defines the contribution of each supplier in contributing towards the delivery of a single, integrated set of services.

The current business trend, however, appears to be towards the management of a greater range of individual contracts over shorter periods, perhaps reflecting the growing risk appetite of many organizations in the pursuit of more economical models, and perhaps a growing desire by customer organizations to reduce the bargaining power of large outsourcers, and avoid being held to ransom by a monopoly supplier.

Some customers have attempted to combine both worlds by awarding a single contract to a consortium of service providers with provision to replace or withdraw services and their providers during the life of the contract. This keeps the bargaining power with the customer and simplifies the contract management, while encouraging a 'best of breed' match of providers to services.

In practice, a lack of attention to relationship management is likely to be the major source of risk in multi-sourcing arrangements, especially those that allow the outsourcers to assume a significant degree of empowerment. The starting assumption for any new supplier should always be that, unless firsthand experience suggests otherwise, the contractor will only deliver what is clearly specified and monitored. Over time, an increasing degree of trust in the outsourcers can be built up; but it would be naïve to assume too high a level of trust from the outset.

3.6.3 Empowerment is a double-edged sword

Some of the most successful outsourcing arrangements are those in which a supplier is both competent and trusted to assume a broader role in, for example, managing a complete end-to-end process in the business value chain. Such a relationship is likely to deliver a greater degree of added value by unleashing the supplier's potential to contribute their more specialist know-how to optimize business processes, and thereby deliver continuous improvement across the business supply chain.

Such partnerships, however, cannot be established overnight. They require time and proactive alignment of the objectives of all parties, as well as a close attention to relationship management at all levels across the partnership. In the absence of a programme of such proactive relationship management, it is unlikely that such a relationship can flourish.

Unsupervised outsourced activities present a dangerous cocktail of risks, some of which can evolve unnoticed until it is too late to mitigate them effectively. In fact, the larger the degree of empowerment, the greater the potential business gains are likely to be when the partnership is managed well. But, on the opposite side of the coin, the business and security risks will be greater when the relationship is managed badly.

3.7 Offshored services

3.7.1 Location makes a difference

Offshoring is a form of outsourcing. (Indeed, in the US the term 'outsourcing' is often used to describe offshoring.) By definition, offshoring implies a transfer of work to an overseas location, usually with the aim of achieving a significant cost saving. It also presents a number of major challenges. In addition to the obvious difficulty in managing a portfolio of business services from a distance, offshoring introduces new business risks, including the possibility of cultural or language misunderstandings, foreign exchange losses (or gains) and, in many cases, a risk of greater political instability.

There are also important legal considerations if any of the data involved is subject to data protection legislation. UK organizations, for example, that outsource business services outside of Europe will need to take account of the special provisions of the Data Protection Act, which prohibits the transfer of personal information outside the European Economic Area unless there is an adequate level of protection for the information, as well as for the affected individuals' rights in relation to that information. Relocation of services or data to another legal jurisdiction can also have a significant impact on legal disclosure requirements or on the conduct of security investigations.

3.7.2 Risks introduced by location change

In fact, any major change in physical or technical environment is likely to have an impact on the security risk profile of an information system or business application. There might be new forms of local physical security threat, changes in security countermeasures, new sources of insider threat, and risks arising from a loss of existing staff experience or perhaps from the move of data to a new regulatory compliance environment.

Physical and environmental threats are significantly different in many popular offshore locations, with higher risks of earthquakes, storms and floods, as well as a greater likelihood of strikes, conflicts and unanticipated regulatory changes. Organizations planning to offshore should consider carefully the full impact of the new environment, including the ability to obtain competent local services to conduct audits, support incident management or assist with security investigations.

Language and culture can also present new forms of risk through possible misunderstandings or misinterpretations of customer demands. Information security is a relatively new discipline, and some emerging concepts and terminology might not translate as intended to other cultures.

The outcome of local risk assessments, for example, might be quite different, because of differences in risk perception, experience, accepted practice, or availability of countermeasures. For that reason, among others, offshoring generally requires a more prescriptive approach to specifications than is desirable for other forms of outsourcing. That in turn demands more attention to detail, especially concerning security requirements, specifications, service reviews, audits and acceptance tests, in order to confirm that the services and products delivered will meet business and security expectations.

It's also important to look ahead at the future economic and business consequences. Offshoring might seem attractive today, but the cost savings are likely to become less significant over time with the growing cost of labour in popular offshore service locations. Exchange rate movements can also have a substantial impact on the competitiveness of offshore services, for better or for worse.

3.7.3 A changing global landscape

Many leading outsourcers have also become increasing global in their service delivery processes, blurring the distinction between many sources of onshore and offshore services. Leading Western and Eastern outsourcers now offer very similar service portfolios at competitive prices. New terms such as near-shoring and right-shoring have also been introduced to reflect the fact that offshoring is now a less clear-cut option for reducing costs. They reflect a change of thinking away from the traditional assumption that overseas sourcing is automatically cheaper and therefore more compelling.

The increasing experience of both customer and service organizations in managing offshore services is, however, helping to mitigate many of the business and security risks associated with offshoring. But offshoring will always remain an option that presents challenging operational risks that will demand greater attention to detail in both the specification of services and the day-to-day management of the services being delivered.

3.8 Cloud computing services

Cloud computing is an emerging approach to IT service delivery that exploits the growing power of networks and virtualization technology to deliver low-cost, scalable computing services. Cloud services can offer substantial cost and efficiency benefits for user organizations, but there are many security and commercial risks associated with the reliance on an external, Internet-based supplier to deliver critical or sensitive business services.

As we enter the second decade of the 21st Century, cloud computing seems as mature as outsourcing might have appeared two decades previously. Various models are being advocated and deployed, but it is likely that not all services or implementations will succeed. Some consolidation is likely in the marketplace. Indeed, it is already clear that IT industry giants such as Microsoft and Amazon are already aiming to dominate the field and dictate the winning solutions.

Jay Heiser, a Gartner security analyst, uses the analogy of a cracked egg to describe the sudden change from a traditional, perimeter-protected IT service provision to an external, distributed, cloud computing service. This image is intended to underline the fragile nature of legacy information systems, few of which were originally designed to be operated securely outside of a dedicated, private environment. However, this analogy is not strictly correct as, unlike a broken egg, it is possible to recreate the original security perimeter of an information system – for example, if the security risks associated with operating within an open environment are considered to be excessive.

Cloud computing services come in various shapes and sizes, ranging from low-level infrastructure services to high-level business applications. The services can be delivered in a variety of forms: they can be public, private or shared across a trusted business community. Each approach presents a different set of considerations and risks, which are analysed in more detail in Chapter 11, which is dedicated to the subject of cloud computing.

An important point to note, however, is that unlike most outsourcing initiatives, which can be highly personalized, cloud computing services are generally based on the provision of larger-scale shared services, offering considerably less scope for individual due diligence, specification of services or negotiation of terms and conditions.

3.9 Learning points from this chapter

This chapter has explored different forms of outsourcing and offshoring arrangement. Key learning points to note can be summarized as follows.

▶ Outsourcing is something obtained by contract from an outside supplier. It can be moving an existing service outside or sourcing a new service externally. The range of tasks contracted out to third parties is growing as the marketplace for external services matures. Outsourcing requires careful planning to manage the risks associated with the transfer of sensitive data or services. The cost of this must be factored into the business case.

▶ Contracts can differ in breadth, depth and granularity, each presenting different security problems, risks and cultural challenges. The scope can be a business process, a set of services or an organizational function, delivered through dedicated, private infrastructure or shared with other customers. Multi-sourcing is increasing, and presents a major challenge for relationship management.

▶ Outsourcing affects the size, shape and role of the security function and other in-house functions, as well as the design and operation of key corporate processes including risk management, business continuity and regulatory compliance. Security services can also be successfully outsourced.

▶ Any subcontracting of services to third parties introduces security risks, including failures, theft, espionage and sabotage. Contractors have increasing access to corporate networks and business data. They have to be trusted, but none should be assumed to be perfect. Evidence of appropriate checks in managing contractors is needed to defend against accusations of negligence. Regulators are increasingly recognising and demanding attention to security controls in the supply chain.

▶ Empowerment of contractors is a double-edged sword. It delivers greater added value but presents a larger set of business and security risks. Contractors working on behalf of the organization must be given a clear statement of their security obligations. A business manager should be assigned to 'own' the contractual relationship and supervise access to buildings and systems.

▶ Offshoring adds the further dimension of a change in location. Any significant change to the business operating environment will result in a significant impact on risk profiles, governance arrangements and compliance processes. Offshoring introduces new risks, including cultural, economic, political, physical and legals risks.

▶ Data protection legislation prohibits transfer of personal information outside Europe, unless citizen rights and data are adequately protected. Differences in language and culture present risks from misunderstandings or misinterpretation. Local risk assessments can also be affected by differences in risk perception, experience, accepted practice, and availability of countermeasures.

▶ Cloud computing is an emerging approach to IT service delivery that exploits the power of networks and virtualization technology to deliver low-cost, scalable computing services. Cloud services offer cost and efficiency benefits but present new security and commercial risks.

▶ Cloud computing comes in various shapes and sizes, ranging from low-level infrastructure services to high-level business applications, which can be public, private or shared across a trusted business community. Each approach presents different considerations and risks. Such services are generally large-scale shared services, offering less scope for specification and inspection of services, and negotiation of terms and conditions.

4 Business drivers for outsourcing

4.1 How business motives shape security expectations

This chapter explores the range of business drivers for outsourcing and their implications for security. Organizations have many different business motives for entering into an outsourcing or offshoring relationship. These underlying motives need to be recognized and addressed when building a security strategy for outsourcing, because they will undoubtedly shape the management criteria for vendor selection, set the tone for the conduct of the relationship, and ultimately determine both the quality and flexibility of the services delivered.

Business motives for outsourcing will have a major influence on the style and effectiveness of the overall security management processes. An enterprise that wishes to build a long-term partnership, for example, will usually aim to develop a relatively light, 'hands-off' management style. In contrast, one that is determined to ruthlessly drive down costs will generally prefer to adopt a more prescriptive 'command and control' approach to the governance of the relationship.

Security expectations regarding the strength and range of the security features, resources and controls provided by the vendor also need to be consistent with the business objectives of outsourcing. Major security improvements cannot be expected from a contractor that has been tasked to cut service costs or deliver services against a reducing business demand. On the other hand, a contractor that aims to increase the level of business done with a customer will be more inclined to assign its best staff and apply its best endeavours to the partnership.

Similarly, if the business driver is to achieve access to a broader pool of skills, then there might well be opportunities to achieve an improvement in the delivery of security activities, especially if the outsourcer can provide a broader view of security threats and best practices from its potentially wider perspective of risks, incidents and ways of working.

Security objectives need to be aligned, as realistically as possible, with the underpinning business drivers in order to avoid disappointment through underachievement, and prevent the consequential misunderstandings, tension and conflict that this is likely to generate.

4.2 Common business motives for outsourcing

A successful relationship needs to be built on realistic targets, an appreciation of the available skills, and recognition of budget and resource constraints. The following examples illustrate the key implications, risks and potential security benefits associated with a range of particular outsourcing motives. Each outsourcing situation is unique but in most cases the primary business drivers for outsourcing and offshoring are likely to be one, or more, of the following objectives:

- cost savings;
- headcount reduction;
- moving to a variable cost basis;
- access to a broader skills base;
- managing legacy systems and infrastructure;
- moving data or processes to a new platform;
- building a global support capability;
- achieving global network leadership;
- gaining a quality improvement.

Each of these business drivers will have a different degree of influence on both the constraints and opportunities for implementing security features, controls and governance. These motives and their consequences for security are examined in the following paragraphs.

4.3 Cost savings

Achieving a reduction in annual spending on business services is perhaps the most significant of all the major business benefits offered by outsourcing and offshoring. Indeed, if the overall service costs were not significantly cheaper, then it would be unlikely that an executive board would even contemplate such a potentially disruptive and distracting business initiative.

Certainly the primary benefit from offshoring of business services is generally financial: the ability to exploit a lower-cost pool of labour offered by many developing countries. But not all savings and costs are equivalent. Gains today do not always compensate for much larger costs tomorrow, though they will certainly present an attractive vehicle for helping to meet or exceed current scorecard targets.

Business drivers for outsourcing

Outsourcers can also offer potential economies of scale and greater purchasing power, though such benefits will not be fully realized unless it is feasible to integrate the outsourced services with the supplier's existing infrastructure. In many cases, the systems and services of a large customer will continue for many years to operate within a dedicated silo of existing skills, resources and facilities within the outsourcer's broader infrastructure. And exploiting the supplier's economies of scale will not only demand radical change, it will also introduce new security risks to the established operating environment.

By taking a longer-term view of revenue and costs, outsourcers can afford to offer attractive rates to customers in the initial years of a contract. Outsourcing offers the potential for significant short-term savings from reduced service costs, as well as a major cash injection through the sale of corporate IT assets to the outsourcer.

Because of this short-term sacrifice by the outsourcer the contract is also highly likely to involve a commitment to much higher service costs in later years, as well as a potential set of cost penalties for addressing unanticipated future changes. These are, in fact, the normal commercial risks associated with the uncertainty surrounding future levels of service demand, as well as the limited ability of the outsourcer to respond to major changes in service requirements.

What is different and special about security requirements is that they are much more likely than routine business requirements to change quickly, and in particular, to progressively increase in future years. Long-term freezing of business specifications in the pursuit of short-term financial gains is generally a bad idea from a security perspective.

Offshoring exploits an economic phenomenon called labour arbitrage, in which work moves to lower-cost nations as a result of improved global communications and the progressive erosion of international trade barriers. Some countries competing for investment might also offer tax incentives to entice overseas companies to establish local business operations.

The savings from cheap labour, even in the short term, will also have to be traded off against any associated tariffs or management overheads, as well as the cultural and financial impact of managing the change. There are also a range of new business risks to be managed: the transfer of the sourcing of services to a new location, ranging from possible shifts (either positive or negative) in currency exchange rates through to the potential impact of political instability, or perhaps regional conflicts or wars.

The main implication for security is the recognition that an organization that is prepared to accept longer-term risks in the pursuit of short-term cost savings has consciously adopted a higher risk appetite in the pursuit of more immediate business goals. Security risks will need to be considered in that light, and potential risks carefully analysed to determine whether the risks are in fact manageable or whether the consequences are deemed unacceptable. Potential 'showstoppers' need to be carefully assessed as, in practice, few security concerns are likely to be sufficiently compelling to persuade an executive board to delay or abandon a decision to proceed with outsourcing simply on the basis of an elevated security risk profile.

The goal of a major cost saving will also have a significant influence on the criteria for vendor selection as well as the anticipated quality of bids offered by potential contractors. In a competition decided primarily on price, security will need to be established as a minimum level of requirement to be met by all bidders to avoid a situation in which the cheapest bid becomes the likely winner, regardless of the level of security presented by the contractor.

But one thing is certainly guaranteed, and that is that the risks, consequences and costs of any underestimation of effort, or overestimation of technology performance, will fall to the outsourcer. The downside of this, however, is that the outsourcer will suffer financially, impacting their capability to deliver services. The truth is that cost savings are easily achievable from outsourcing initiatives, but this target will generally be accompanied by an increased degree of risk.

4.4 Headcount reduction

Reducing headcount has been an imperative for most organizations for at least the past two decades, as business process re-engineering and other organizational development initiatives have pointed the way towards increasingly lean management structures. Reducing the in-house workforce also reduces the amount of spending per manager, as well as increasing the perceived value generated per employee, which is a key business metric that is likely to impress investors and market analysts.

The outcome of this thinking has been the encouragement of frequent downsizing exercises, as well as strict target-setting for manpower budgets and staff complements. In recent years, recessionary pressures have also played a major part in fuelling a more urgent desire to reduce in-house staff, especially as the value of middle managers is not only hard to articulate, but also questionable in an increasingly networked business environment.

Outsourcing is often the easiest and most practical means for a business unit or a corporate function to achieve a large-scale headcount reduction without a major impact on services. Unfortunately, it is often the case that the middle managers manage the much-needed governance aspects across the essential business services and supply chains.

When headcount reduction is the major driver behind an outsourcing exercise, the major security issue is generally the size of the core team that remains behind to define the business requirements and manage the contract. The optimum size of the retained team depends on many factors, including the management structure of the consortium delivering the services and the complexity of the service portfolio.

Clearly, a multi-sourced contract involving several specialist contractors will be much more demanding to manage than a single consortium led by a prime contractor. The structure and the maturity in outsourcing of the customer management function will also play a significant part in the decision on which in-house resources to let go, and which to retain.

Organizations that have previously established external governance processes through earlier experience of outsourcing are generally in a much better position to manage a complex outsourcing contract with a small, experienced team of support staff. Enterprises that are new to outsourcing, however, will have to design and implement many new processes to manage the contract and monitor the delivery of services, requiring, at least initially, a much larger in-house team.

The major issue for security in outsourcing contracts that aim to reduce headcount is the need to establish a viable dividing line and efficient operational interface between the security activities carried out by the outsourcer and the ones to be retained in-house. Contractors cannot be left to assume and manage security risks that might have a major impact on the user organization.

Yet, at the same time, it has to be recognized that the in-house function will have considerably less visibility and control of the risks associated with day-to-day business operations. The size and role of the in-house security function should therefore be carefully assessed before implementation, and its performance monitored during the early months of operation to ensure that excessive headcount reductions do not result in an ineffective security management system or introduce any unacceptable new security risks.

One important overriding consideration, however, is that regardless of the economic temptations to shed staff, accountability for the consequences of data breaches will always remain firmly with the customer organization. You can externalize tasks and jobs, but you can't outsource the responsibility for dealing with a major security breach.

4.5 Moving to a variable cost basis

In the past, many traditional in-house functions accumulated surprisingly high percentages of fixed costs based on long-term investments in staff, equipment and premises. The result of this is that any reductions in the demand for products or services will not translate into significant cost savings. This situation might well be tolerable in a business environment that is constantly expanding, but in mature markets and times of recession it will become a visible business overhead.

From this perspective, outsourcing is an attractive option as it helps to convert fixed in-house costs to variable and potentially more predictable external rates. In economic terms, it transforms the operating leverage of a company, enabling a more direct translation of revenue growth (or loss) into an operating income.

Organizations anticipating a major downsizing of staff, or simply a drop in customer demand or production, will clearly benefit from a switch to a service provider offering a variable rate based on actual demand levels rather than a fixed set of costs. This arrangement will work very well where services are shared across multiple customers, enabling the results of individual fluctuations in demand to be evened out. In a dedicated service environment, however, based on a single customer and supplier, such a deal will create a potential zero-sum game in which one party benefits at the expense of the other, resulting in an adversarial relationship.

There is also the possibility of a contractor miscalculating demand and, as a consequence, suffering a major loss. In an unexpected recession, such a strategy might result in reducing demand levels for a service from a large proportion of customers, leading to serious financial difficulties, reduced quality of services and, in the worse cases, potential bankruptcy for the outsourcer.

In fact, a move to a variable cost model is likely to be characterized by a range of commercial risks, which is likely in many cases to set the tone for a more formal, perhaps confrontational, relationship. This will also have a potential impact on the cost model for any outsourced security services, discouraging the outsourcer's staff from going the extra mile in the interests of security.

Achieving a successful model for a variable cost model is far from easy. It requires a tight, formal specification of outsourced security services that will be less of a hostage to unanticipated changes. In today's business environment, however, which is characterized by unanticipated swings in business demand and fast-changing, evolving security threats and exposures, this is likely to prove to be a major challenge.

4.6 Access to a broader skills base

The fast-changing nature of our IT industry can result in many organizations accumulating an increasing proportion of legacy skills and experience at the expense of emerging ones. This is a problem that is not restricted to the IT or security industries. The same phenomenon can also be seen in fast-moving business areas such as financial services, where new products and techniques are constantly emerging.

The solution for many organizations is to move to an outsourced services model to ensure ready access to the range of skills and experience needed to respond to new business opportunities. Outsourcing can address this problem space quite well. But customers should be under no illusions. What might seem possible in theory might not be easily achievable in practice.

Many outsourcing organizations are composed primarily from the results of an ad hoc collection of inherited outsourced staff from previous contracts. Such resources might prove to be no more capable or up-to-date than a customer organization's existing in-house IT function. Outsourcers might appear at first sight to possess an impressive range of specialist staff with in-depth and in-demand expertise, but these resources might not be readily available to every customer. Many skilled resources are likely to be subject to an internal market of competing customers, in which only the highest bids succeed in securing the services of the 'top talent'.

Outsourcing customers frequently complain of being landed with a 'B' or 'C' team of contractors, following a highly impressive pitch by an 'A' team of experts assigned to the initial bid. This is simply a hard fact of commercial life. You will get what you pay for. Customers should concentrate on the quality of the deliverables, of course, rather than the capabilities of the supplier's resources, but the two are clearly related. Ensuring access to the best skills demands smart, proactive management of the contract, requiring a focus on the value of the output. This might involve a greater up-front investment, rather than just the cost of the service.

The consequences for security, however, can be much better when access to skills is the primary driving force for the outsourcing initiative, because it helps to encourage the selected supplier to maintain a broad range of resources with up-to-date and emerging skills, which is vital in developing solutions to challenging new security problems. The major problem to address, however, is to ensure that the supplier's expertise is available not only within the company, but in particular to your contract whenever you might need it.

In a relatively new profession such as security, where training and experience are in short supply, it makes sense every now and then to take a step back and contemplate which activities can continue to be adequately resourced in-house, and which ones might best be outsourced to an outsourcer or an independent third-party supplier with a broader skill base.

Such a decision might seem harsh on valued in-house professionals, but many might have better prospects for their professional development with a larger service provider. And there are likely to be many major changes in the skills and experience required in future security professionals. But achieving the right combination of in-house security staff for an outsourcing arrangement is far from easy. In-house staff cannot easily assess the day-to-day risks associated with a portfolio of remotely managed services, nor control the selection of countermeasures or the management of incidents. They will be assumed to be accountable for all incidents, though relatively powerless to intervene in many cases.

On the other hand, outsourced security managers have limited understanding of business risks and the impact of breaches, yet their day-to-day decisions will have a major influence on the resulting risk profile. The ideal solution is to aim to build an effective 'virtual team' that can share knowledge and skills and apply them seamlessly to any situation. This is far from easy to achieve in practice because of political, financial and operational constraints, but it is much more likely to be achievable in an environment in which the primary business driver is access to a broader skills base.

4.7 Managing legacy systems and infrastructure

One well-established driver for selective outsourcing is the difficulty and growing expense of supporting essential legacy systems and infrastructure. Over time, legacy systems and infrastructure tend to become increasingly expensive and difficult to maintain. Economies of scale in managing services reduce with falling user demand. Specialist support staff also become harder to recruit and less compelling to employ. These factors make it difficult to maintain aging legacy systems in-house, and encourage many customer organizations to seek support from more specialized external service providers.

In fact, proactive identification and outsourcing of legacy systems is a sensible idea, as such systems rarely cry out for major changes until they break down or the business product they support becomes uncompetitive. The longer they are deployed, the more expensive the service costs tend to become, and the less money is available to cover the costs of major changes or migration to a new platform or system.

Outsourcing to a specialist third-party provider is a sensible strategic move, though it also introduces an obvious risk to customers of the outsourcer being able to maintain a portfolio of obsolescent systems at competitive market prices. It is important, therefore, to ensure that the outsourcer has a realistic business model that is based on more than a short-term, profitable peak demand, and is also capable of achieving growing margins of revenue and income throughout a period of declining future demand.

The major security risks when legacy systems are outsourced to externalize the cost and difficulty of supporting them are, unsurprisingly, in the area of business continuity management. Vendors that specialize in legacy system support will generally be aiming to succeed on the basis of declining competition for provision of services, enabling a growing portfolio of customers to support business growth targets as the choice of alternative service providers dwindles.

Customers in this situation should constantly review the marketplace for signs of over-dependency on a single supplier, which presents a major risk to business continuity in the event of a service failure by the outsourcer. The alternative option will be to ensure that a minimal but adequate capability is retained in-house to cater for potential service failures, including the prospect of the vendor withdrawing the service because of falling customer demand.

4.8 Moving data or processes to a new platform

A further business driver for outsourcing is to enable the migration of business data and processes from legacy systems and infrastructure to a new set of platforms. This option is attractive to many customer organizations, as it avoids high capital investment funds and the need for specialist in-house skills and resources. It also enables development and operating costs to be spread over a longer term.

The security implications for establishing a new set of platforms are generally positive. New systems and platforms are often a change for the better, from a security perspective. New application systems might lack some of the business controls provided in legacy systems, but newer platforms often provide a richer set of security controls and features, and are less likely to contain the type of longstanding, deep-seated security vulnerabilities that can be encountered in older platforms, designed when security threats were less sophisticated.

The main requirement is to ensure that a suitable security risk assessment is carried out at the outset, and that an appropriate specification of security features and controls is produced.

4.9 Building a global support capability

For an aspiring global business service provider, outsourcing can enable access to a new range of skills that can transcend national and corporate boundaries. This will deliver an efficient portfolio of services to users in remote countries, which might otherwise present a major service challenge for an in-house service provider.

In fact, the growth of the global landscape of outsourcing service providers has been impressive over the last decade as both Eastern and Western outsourcers have built or acquired unprecedented sets of global capabilities, such that it is no longer unusual for a Western service provider to win large contracts in the East, or for an Eastern company to win major outsourcing contracts in the West. The maturity of the marketplace is such that experienced suppliers from both sides of the world can now offer global services at similar rates, delivered to or from anywhere in the world.

Location is now much less important from the supplier's perspective, though it can still present major challenges for security, compliance and due diligence. In particular, the precise location of data and services will influence both the requirements and consequences for regulatory compliance, especially concerning data protection and privacy.

Many laws and regulatory compliance demands vary from country to country, and some can even be contradictory. No outsourcing initiative should proceed, therefore, without a clear understanding of the full implications of any projected or potential future changes to the geographic locations in which sensitive personal data might be stored or processed.

4.10 Achieving global network leadership

Companies adopt different strategies for global business success. Some aim to focus on developing a set of strong, in-house capabilities, enabling them to deliver high-quality products and services. Others aim to develop a world-class commercial management capability, excelling in managing contracts with third-party producers.

Some organizations are initially attracted to outsourcing because they believe that delegating routine support activities to a more competent third party will free up valuable management time, enabling business managers to focus on their key strengths and future strategy. It is an understandable aspiration, though an unlikely outcome. Managing outsourced services demands a highly disciplined approach to services provision.

Lack of attention to the governance of external services is likely to result in a growing set of new management problems and liabilities, which can prove to be an even greater distraction for business managers. In fact, lack of attention to detail during any stage of the outsourcing lifecycle process can lead to failures in service delivery and barriers to innovation and change, which all demand careful planning, negotiation and supervision by the customer.

Companies that rise to the challenge of achieving a highly professional approach to managing outsourced contracts, however, can set their aspirations on the more ambitious target of achieving global network leadership in business partnerships. A capability to manage large, complex portfolios of externalized services efficiently is a precursor for assuming leadership of collaborative business consortia.

Such a business motivation for outsourcing is beneficial to security, as it encourages the establishment of a strong, outward-facing framework of security governance standards and processes. As many other organizations struggle with a half-hearted commitment to a partial outsourcing of business services, companies that set out to build the skills, know-how and processes to manage a fully outsourced set of services can evolve to become future market leaders and virtual security leaders, which are valuable business assets in an increasingly networked, global business environment.

4.11 Gaining a quality improvement

Not every organization is able to deliver the professional level of services that today's competitive business processes and customers demand. For many enterprises, outsourcing offers the potential for achieving a level of quality in professional services delivery that existing in-house services are physically or financially incapable of achieving.

There is, of course, a danger that senior management might automatically, and perhaps falsely, assume that external service providers will naturally be more effective and efficient than existing in-house staff, only to subsequently discover that they are left with the same staff but with lower budgets, or with new staff that have no knowledge of the customer's business requirements and systems.

It is logical to assume that specialist service providers will possess broader and deeper skills and experience. However, as mentioned earlier, many outsourcers will have built much of their capability by absorbing customer staff from previous outsourcing contracts. Such staff will have been inherited rather than cherry-picked from the marketplace, though in most cases they will have come from blue chip organizations. A good outsourcer, however, can draw on a broader set of skills and knowledge, a disciplined approach to service delivery, and a more extensive portfolio of professional management frameworks and support tools.

Moving to an outside service provider, however, presents an opportunity for achieving improvements in service levels through more formal, contractual service-level agreements, with financial penalties and legal redress. Legal redress is reassuring, but it only comes into play in the event of a major failure in support, which is something that all parties should be aiming to avoid.

Nevertheless, the threat of legal action can serve to sharpen the performance of service providers. At the very least, a decision to outsource will remove the inhibitors to improvements that are often associated with in-house monopoly service arrangements. Professional external service providers are also likely to operate more mature systems development processes, based on a higher level of quality management achievement, such as the service marks of the Carnegie-Mellon University Capability Maturity Model.

Large outsourcers are likely to possess an impressive range of intellectual assets, including specialist skills, research, software products, methodologies and a knowledge base. These assets might not, however, be available within the outsourcing arrangement or might come at a high price. Exploiting such intellectual property is far from easy in practice and demands a proactive strategy, which invests time and resources in identifying opportunities and implementing a suitable process of technology transfer.

A more practical approach to business improvement is to exploit the opportunity presented by the introduction of a new partner as a catalyst for change. The injection of a new partner can set the tone and enhance the potential for innovation and new product development. These benefits are especially important for smaller and medium-sized organizations which, through outsourcing, can match the greater capabilities of much larger organizations but with greater business agility and less administrative baggage.

4.12 Learning points from this chapter

This chapter has explored a range of business drivers for outsourcing and their implications for security. Key learning points to note can be summarized as follows.

▶ Organizations have different business motives for outsourcing or offshoring. These motives shape the criteria for vendor selection, the tone of the relationship, and the quality and flexibility of the services delivered. The outcome will be different for an enterprise that wishes to build a long-term partnership, than one determined to drive down costs.

▶ Security expectations need to be consistent with business objectives. Improvements should not be expected when the aim is to cut costs. But partnerships can introduce a broader view of security threats and best practices. A successful relationship needs to be built on realistic targets, an appreciation of the available skills, and recognition of budget and resource constraints.

▶ Common business drivers for outsourcing include cost savings, headcount reduction, achieving a variable cost basis, gaining a broader skills base, maintaining legacy systems, moving to new platforms, building a global support capability, achieving business network leadership, or gaining a quality improvement. Each business driver influences the constraints and opportunities for implementing security.

▶ Cost savings from outsourcing are often short-term gains with a commitment to higher costs in later years. This reflects an implicit adoption of a higher risk appetite. In such cases, security risks need to be carefully analysed to determine whether the risks are manageable and acceptable. The goal of a cost saving will influence the quality of bids. In such cases, a minimum level of security will need to be established.

▶ Outsourcing is an easy means for achieving headcount reduction without loss of services. In such cases, the major security issue is the size of the core team that remains behind to define requirements and manage the contract. The optimum size of this team depends on the management structure of the consortium delivering the services and the complexity of the service portfolio. Jobs can be externalized, but not accountability for the consequences of breaches.

▶ Achieving the right combination of in-house security staff for an outsourcing arrangement is not easy. In-house staff cannot assess the day-to-day risks associated with remotely managed services, nor control the selection of countermeasures or the management of incidents. They will be held accountable for incidents, though powerless to intervene in many cases. Outsourced security managers have limited understanding of business risks and impacts, though their decisions will have a major influence on the risk profile. The ideal solution is to build a 'virtual team' that shares knowledge and skills.

▶ Business continuity is the major risk when legacy systems are outsourced to reduce the cost and difficulty of supporting them. A move to a new platform is generally better. Newer platforms provide better security features, and are less likely to contain deep-seated vulnerabilities.

Business drivers for outsourcing

▶ Companies that adopt a professional approach to managing outsourced contracts are in a better position to assume leadership of collaborative business consortia. Such a motivation is beneficial to security, encouraging a strong, outward-facing governance framework.

▶ Outsourcing also presents opportunities for improvements in service levels through formal, contractual agreements with financial penalties and legal redress. Legal redress is reassuring, but reflects a breakdown in the relationship, which should be avoided as far as possible.

▶ A new partnership can be a catalyst for change, enhancing the potential for innovation and new product development. It can enable smaller organizations to match the capabilities of larger organizations, but with greater agility and less administrative baggage.

5 Planning and preparation

5.1 Security throughout the outsourcing lifecycle

5.1.1 The importance of early planning

As with any major business improvement project, good advance planning and preparation is the first and arguably the most important step in the process of outsourcing or offshoring. In particular, the planning phase is the critical point for identifying major security risks and requirements, as these findings will serve to inform senior business management of consequential security issues, compliance considerations and implementation or operational overheads that might not have been factored into the initial consideration of the business case for outsourcing.

In fact, security, compliance and risk considerations need to be addressed at all stages of the outsourcing lifecycle, from initial conception right through to final termination of contract. As with any major change programme, there will always be a degree of uncertainty at the outset about the full consequences of the change, but this will progressively lessen throughout each phase of the programme.

The business case for the change is likely to change during the early stages, generally becoming progressively negative as overlooked costs tend to come to light, whereas new benefits or savings rarely emerge. This can lead to political pressure to move quickly or freeze specifications in order to avoid mounting costs.

From a security perspective, however, one thing is certain. It will become harder and more expensive to address security risks and compliance issues, the later they are identified, assessed and addressed.

5.1.2 Key decision points

Later chapters of this book will set out in more detail the security considerations that need to be taken into account, in a logical sequence based on the outsourcing lifecycle. But there are several key decision points worth noting that require an informed security input.

1) At the outset, when a firm decision is made to proceed with an outsourcing or offshoring initiative. At this point the most likely sources of risk and the broad consequences and costs for security will need to be taken into account.
2) At the definition stage, when the precise scope of the IT systems or business services to be outsourced is determined. The key security inputs at this stage are the security needs of critical and sensitive information in scope.
3) During the planning and selection stage when proposals are invited and considered from potential contractors. At this stage policies and standards need to be clearly defined, and appropriate due diligence carried out on bidders.
4) Through the development and negotiation phases of the contract, when a range of contract schedules relating to security, risk management, audit and compliance will need to be defined and agreed.
5) When implementing the new outsourcing or offshoring arrangements, at which point many new security arrangements and governance processes will need to be jointly developed and put in place.
6) When considering future changes, including the longer-term need to review, renegotiate, terminate or exit from the outsourcing or offshoring arrangement. At this stage the implications for security, such as the need to return or destroy intellectual property, will need to be considered.

5.1.3 Security objectives in the outsourcing lifecycle

The key security objectives at the various stages in the outsourcing lifecycle are illustrated in Figure 2. Each stage involves a different set of security activities, ranging from identification, review and definition of requirements through to management of operational security activities.

The lifecycle begins by aligning security objectives with business objectives and establishing the risk profiles of the systems and assets within scope. It ends with prudent management of operational activities, including the return or assured destruction of all business information and other intellectual assets held by the outsourcer at the termination of the contract.

5.2 Strategic considerations

Planning and preparation is arguably the most important phase of an outsourcing or offshoring programme, as it sets out the vision and strategy for the delivery

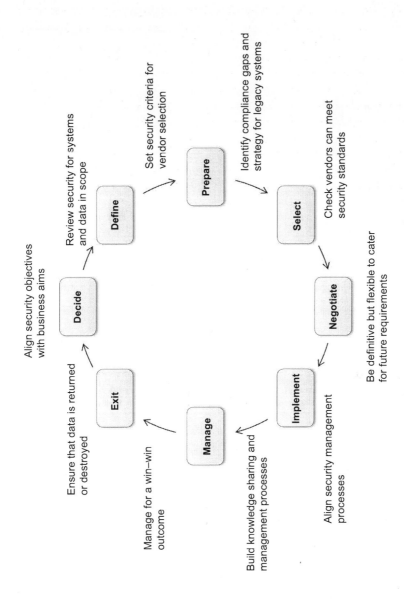

Figure 2 – Security objectives in stages of the outsourcing lifecycle

of the services within scope, identifies and considers the associated risks, costs and benefits, and determines the activities, time and resources needed to deliver the vision. Done properly, it will ensure that the following phases are properly resourced, and that the organization enters the outsourcing programme fully briefed as to the full implications.

The starting point for any organization planning an outsourcing initiative is to identify and assess the likely costs, benefits and risks that will ensue. I use the word 'likely' because at this initial stage it will not be possible to know the exact prices that will be offered by potential bidders, who will need to conduct their own analysis of the customer's requirements before presenting a proposal. Nor will it be possible to establish the full costs of the exercise without first carrying out a comprehensive analysis of the many changes involved and their implications for staffing and security.

ISO/IEC 27036, an emerging International Standard for managing security in outsourcing, sets out a number of key elements that an organization should take into consideration when deciding whether or not to undertake outsourcing. These include

- the organization's needs related to outsourcing,
- senior management sponsorship; in particular a commitment to establish the necessary scope and strategic perspective for the outsourcing activities,
- anticipated benefits,
- critical success factors,
- legal constraints; in particular the identification of the standards and regulations laid down by regulatory authorities to determine the constraints that impact the outsourcing activities,
- an information security framework applied at the organizational level, and
- unacceptable risks, establishing the minimum circumstances in which the outsourcing initiative should be abandoned.

The standard recommends that the outsourcing strategy is defined as clearly as possible, in order to provide a sensible basis for analysis and discussion, and to ensure alignment with the organization's information security governance and corporate strategy.

If the outline business case appears to be compelling, then the next stage will be to identify the activities required to take the initiative forward. From a security perspective, there are several key activities that will need to be addressed at the planning and preparation stage in order to ensure that appropriate protection will be afforded to the organization's assets following the transfer of control to the outsourcer.

1) Establish the precise scope of the outsourcing.
2) Classify sensitive, critical or valuable intellectual assets to enable security attention and activities to be prioritized.
3) Conduct a risk assessment to identity the most significant security risks, their probability and business impact.
4) Review security policies, architecture and standards to ensure they are current and appropriate.

The key constraint in achieving the above will be the limited time and resources available to conduct a comprehensive analysis. This implies the need for some form of prioritization based on the sensitivity, criticality or value of the assets at risk, as well as the relative size of the associated security risks.

5.3 Reviewing the scope of the outsourcing

The first major security activity should be to establish the scope of the proposed outsource and to identify the range of valuable, critical and sensitive data assets that are within scope. There are three compelling reasons for this. Firstly, to enable you to understand the size and extent of the risks and potential business impact associated with the proposed outsourcing. Secondly, to help identify legal and regulatory compliance requirements that might have a bearing on the conditions of the outsourcing arrangement. And thirdly, to identify the need for any exceptional security measures that need to be addressed in the outsourcing contract schedules.

This task should not be underestimated, however. Few organizations have accurate, up-to-date inventories of all systems and assets. Even fewer have up-to-date risk profiles for their critical or sensitive applications and data. Most outsourcing initiatives involve a range of sensitive personal data, especially if they involve HR or customer relationship management processes.

It is essential to carry out a review to determine which applications or services might warrant additional security protection. It is likely in many cases that the level of protection deemed appropriate might be above the level normally offered by the outsourcer. In some cases, it might even be above the level currently being applied by the in-house service provider. Legacy security measures can be expensive to upgrade following an outsourcing. It is important, therefore, to identify the need for improvements or additional countermeasures at the earliest possible stage in the procurement process.

Key questions to ask about the data that falls within scope might include the following.

- What sensitive data is in scope?
- Does any of the data fall within the scope of data protection legislation or the Payment Card Industry Data Security Standard?
- Who is responsible for this data? And have they been consulted about the initiative to outsource?
- Which parties will in future decide the purposes, scope and location for processing personal data?
- Is it legal to hand over this data to a third-party vendor?
- In which jurisdictions will the data reside, and what are the legal implications of that?
- What legal and security measures will be necessary to safeguard this data?
- Are there any transferred responsibilities which might make the vendor a data controller from a data protection perspective, thereby introducing new responsibilities?
- If a consortium is involved, is it clear who is responsible for safeguarding sensitive personal data?

The scope of personal data can be surprisingly large. It can extend to names, addresses, email addresses, family connections, business contacts, personnel records, performance reviews, photographs, CCTV footage and more. Such data is likely to extend across many systems and services. The scope of sensitive personal data is also quite varied, including, for example, medical records, social security details, background checks, trade union memberships, religion and more. Such data needs to be controlled very strictly. Data quality is also an issue, as it currently attracts little attention despite being a common weakness in many customer databases.

The key consideration in examining the scope and answering questions such as the above is the limited amount of time that is likely to be available to develop the plan, specification and contract for the outsourcing programme. There are pragmatic reasons for moving quickly, as business cases for outsourcing tend to become increasingly negative the longer the exercise continues. This is because as the programme progresses many overlooked costs will come to light, whereas overlooked savings are much fewer and far between. Most business cases for new IT investments are optimistic, a tendency that is regularly confirmed by post-implementation audits of IT projects.

Many people might believe that projects can be speeded up without loss of quality by an injection of additional resources. But not every activity can be accelerated. As Fred Brooks, a computer scientist once put it: 'The bearing of a child takes nine months, no matter how many women are assigned.' When time is tight, we should expect neither perfection nor complete coverage of the problem space. Unless the applications portfolio is very small, it will prove unfeasible to properly catalogue all systems, platforms and data, simply because of time and resource restrictions. Just finding out what is actually in place can be a major challenge in itself. It's not unusual for large organizations to overlook hundreds of items when outsourcing a major slice of their IT estate. Further systems and assets are likely to come to light during the outsourcing process.

Modern 'discovery' technologies can help to identify assets connected to corporate networks and to help map data flows. But prioritization is the key. Start with the most valuable, critical and sensitive systems and assets, before proceeding to examine the less important ones. Rank them in order of significance, so that the most important items are guaranteed attention before time and resources run out.

In practice it's not as easy as it might sound to define and rank information assets, as different people will have varying levels of knowledge about the nature of the IT estate, as well as different perceptions of which systems or services are the most important. Compiling such a list requires a clear, objective set of criteria, as well as a team effort between business application owners, systems managers and security personnel.

5.4 Classifying information assets

5.4.1 The need for classification

Information security classifications are a powerful tool for differentiating information or systems that require exceptional security treatment. They are also a blunt instrument that 'shoehorns' items of data into a small number of divisions, which might not reflect their individual requirements. In an ideal world it would be more satisfactory to treat each piece of information as a unique entity, but that would be both unmanageable and expensive.

Classifications are needed to simplify complex decision processes. Their main disadvantage is that whenever we label an item of data with a security classification, we tend to freeze its perceived value, as well as the rules that determine its handling. But the value or utility of a piece of information is not static. It changes with use, and over time, and it is more often in the 'eye of the beholder', presenting a different perceived value to different stakeholders.

When designing a classification system for information assets, it's important to aim for the most efficient balance between *richness* and *simplicity*. There are numerous categories and adjectives used to describe data which, if lost or corrupted, could cause significant business damage. In the past, confidentiality of data was the sole basis of most security classification schemes. In recent years this has been extended to other characteristics of information.

Defining levels of confidentiality might sound like a simple concept requiring an uncomplicated measurement scale, but this can easily escalate. Government security agencies have taken this concept to quite an extreme level of sophistication, engineering complex schemes to protect their secrets. The range of labels used can be quite extensive. In addition to the well-known national security classifications of 'Restricted', 'Confidential', 'Secret' and 'Top Secret',[4] most governments have adopted a wide range of alternative protective markings such as 'Commercial in Confidence', as well as caveats such as 'Eyes Only', and extensive lists of code words such as 'Ultra', to protect individual sources of intelligence. A single item of classified intelligence material might attract as many as four different labels.

Industry has largely taken a much simpler approach to confidentiality, adopting a single label with two or three variants to describe different levels of sensitivity. Existing security classification systems are a good starting point for identifying and highlighting assets that warrant special treatment or additional protection, though not every organization operates such a scheme, and many quickly fall into disuse or even unintended misuse.

---

[4] The practice of stamping the security marking 'Secret' or 'Confidential' on military documents goes back to the end of the 19th Century with the passage of the British Official Secrets Act. By the middle of the 20th Century this had expanded to include 'Restricted' and 'Most Secret', which was eventually changed to 'Top Secret' in agreement with US Government authorities.

Historically, classification schemes in industry were first adopted either by defence contractors to satisfy government demands, or by companies with research laboratories and trade secrets that needed formal, legal protection. It's worth noting that a functioning information classification system, not just a published policy, is needed to provide adequate legal protection of trade secrets, as several companies have found to their cost when attempting to defend their interests in court. A complex scheme is not required, however, to provide such legal protection. In fact, a single label and set of rules is all that is needed for this particular purpose.

Security classification labels are useful for other things besides protecting national security interests and trade secrets. They are generally intended to convey a minimum standard of protection based on a related level of damage, but they can also be used to control the dissemination of information, for example for information management purposes.

In fact, labelling systems can be extended to address many aspects of information management and reflect many different perspectives on the value or utility of information assets, including where it might be processed, or how the sensitivity might change over time. But extensions of this type are not recommended. Two or three labels are more than enough for most managers and users to handle. Simple is best when it comes to designing labels designed for people to recognize and apply.

One major problem with security classification systems, however, is that although the designs of many organizations' schemes are very similar, there remain some subtle differences. Identical-looking labels can have different interpretations across a supply chain. One organization's 'Restricted' information might be the equivalent of another's 'Secret' data. Agreements and guidance must be established to avoid these problems.

A further issue is that the use of classification labels and their associated countermeasures tends to change over time. Classification schemes therefore need periodic adjustment to fine-tune the number of levels, labels, definitions and guidance in protective measures. Regardless of their problems, however, the use of classification systems is growing because they are a powerful tool for communicating policy and rules about the protection of information. And that is something that is especially important for safeguarding sensitive information and valuable intellectual assets across outsourced supply chains.

5.4.2 Identifying classified assets

Information does not always neatly fit into defined categories, so it's not surprising to find that many items do not fit the traditional descriptions used to classify information for security purposes, and cannot easily be identified from the definitions alone. We often loosely apply adjectives such as 'valuable', 'sensitive' and 'critical' to describe items of business data that need protection from threats to their confidentiality, integrity or availability. These words imply a richer view of information security than traditional classification systems usually provide. They also point to the need for a flexible approach to identifying data that warrants exceptional treatment.

Some data, for example, is critical to business operations and creates a major business impact when it becomes corrupted or unavailable. An example of that might be key reference data that controls the execution of a major business process. The word 'critical' is generally used within the context of business continuity management. To identify such data it is better to review each major business process from end to end, i.e. from start to finish, looking for data that is likely to cause a major process failure.

Other data is 'sensitive', in that it might create harm to an individual or organization if compromised. Examples of that might be personal information on customers or employees, or perhaps market-sensitive information about mergers and acquisition. To identify this data it's best to draw up a list of categories of information that is likely to be sensitive to unauthorized or unintended disclosure. However, simple adjectives such as 'sensitive' or 'critical' are not by themselves sufficient to identify an organization's most valuable assets.

There might be other items of information that are neither critical to business operations nor sensitive from a disclosure perspective, but are sufficiently valuable to warrant an additional degree of protection. Examples of that might be data that provides details of major investments, or perhaps an important knowledge base that contributes significantly to overall business efficiency. Such information is perhaps best identified by asking open questions such as, 'What are the crown jewels of the organization?' In fact, what really counts is the resulting business impact of any loss, damage or unauthorized change to data, and that needs to form the basis of the definitions used to classify the data.

Formal classification systems need to be established, with clear definitions, rules and examples of the types of information that might fall into each category. Ideas that can help users to determine the correct classification include the use of financial limits, to express the level of damage that might arise from disclosure, or perhaps target percentages of overall information that are likely to fall into each category. For example, in a large organization we might suggest that the highest level is appropriate for damage greater than one million dollars.

We could also suggest that 'Secret' items should not represent more than 5% of the overall data in a business unit. But such guidance will need to be tailored to the organization, and that demonstrates an unavoidable weakness of security classification systems: one company's minor hit is another's major disaster. Most information has no absolute, universal value. And that in itself is a good reason for ensuring that vendors adhere to the judgements of customers rather than assess the value of a client's data based on their own risk perception.

A further consideration, when undertaking the classification of data, is how to assess the value and sensitivity of any new intellectual property that is generated within the scope of the new partnerships. There are likely to be new methods, systems and databases that are jointly developed to solve customer business problems or implement management processes. Such assets will require legal agreements and will need to be safeguarded from unauthorized exploitation through a security classification system. Key questions to ask are how will such assets be identified, who will 'own' the information, who will control it, and to what standards will it require protection?

5.4.3 Security classification labels

Each organization will have its individual preferences, but examples of commonly used classification labels for safeguarding the confidentiality of information are given below. In the absence of any existing system, these can provide a useful starting point for the design of a simple classification scheme.

'Internal' or 'Restricted'

This label is useful to describe information that can be freely shared with staff, agents or contractors, but not with other third parties except by agreement with the information owner. It will generally apply to information that is likely to cause a degree of embarrassment or negative publicity if made public.

Recipients will be expected to apply a sensible degree of due care and attention to prevent wider, public disclosure, but the information will not justify the need for expensive countermeasures.

'Confidential'

This label is useful to describe information that should only be shared with staff or contractors on a need-to-know basis, because its disclosure might cause significant damage to the interests of the organization or an individual. Examples would include negotiating positions, customer information or sensitive employee data. Such information will require protection from unauthorized access by internal as well external staff. Stronger countermeasures will be required to prevent unauthorized access, such as locked containers, a clear-desk policy, encryption, and the use of non-disclosure agreements when sharing with third parties.

'Secret' or 'Strictly Confidential'

This label is useful to describe information that must be strictly controlled and limited to a minimal list of nominated individuals, because its disclosure might cause serious damage to the interests of the organization. Examples might be details of major acquisitions, investment or mergers, or perhaps forthcoming restructures. The owner or originator of the information will normally be responsible for controlling the dissemination of the information. This information will need to be afforded the highest level of protection available within the business environment.

Labels for integrity and availability

In recent years, as more and more companies have adopted classification schemes, some have also sought to extend them to cover aspects of integrity and availability, the other two fundamental pillars of information security. This is such a new and difficult area that it's hard to identify best or commonly accepted practices either in the choice of labels or in the definitions of information that might fit these categories.

Most schemes tend to use the label 'Critical', which is used in a variety of contexts, for example to describe information that needs to be available at all times, or that needs to be safeguarded against modification. These requirements are generally linked and they can in fact be combined to identify information whose availability and integrity is essential to the execution of critical business activities.

Colour coding

Associating colours with classification levels can be helpful to users, as long as a consistent pattern is chosen. Fortunately, there is a standard, developed initially by the G8 countries and now used by more than 30 countries, to enable dissemination of sensitive information between government agencies and corporations. This 'Traffic Light Protocol' consists of four levels:

Red: personal – for named recipients only, such as those present at a meeting;
Amber: limited distribution within the organization on a need-to-know basis;
Green: community-wide (but not public);
White: unlimited distribution.

This system of colours provides a good, simple starting point for marking documents that flow across organizational boundaries.

5.4.4 Maintaining a register of classified data

In a perfect world we might aim to assign formal ownership, access rights and classification labels to every corporate database and document. But this is an unrealistic goal. It's challenging enough to prompt busy users to place a single classification label on exceptionally sensitive information. We need to limit our ambitions to something that is more achievable in the short term and can be easily maintained over the long term.

Such a solution might be based on a simple register of the most sensitive, critical and valuable information assets, together with an indication of responsibilities and standards of protection. This will require a degree of review of many individual systems and databases. In practice, it is a major challenge to be able to find the time and resources to review and catalogue more than 10% of the overall set of information systems. If you can achieve this, then you're probably doing well. Reviews of security take time and require specialist security advice. Very large, complex application systems can require days or even weeks to review thoroughly.

Information about important assets can be structured in a number of ways: by organizational unit, business process, application system, or geographic location. The simplest and best method is to structure the review by applications portfolios, because this is an efficient, well-established structure for managing IT within the enterprise. Ownership, documentation and controls tend to be focused at the application level, rather than the data or infrastructure level.

Establishing a register or database at this level also opens up the possibility of a degree of convergence between the processes and documentation needed to support information security and those used to manage the applications portfolio. Dedicated databases developed specifically to support an outsourcing programme are generally wasted unless they are regularly used and maintained. Many of us can remember, for example, the inventories of critical systems that were compiled in the late 1990s to support Year 2000 (the so-called 'Millennium Bug') remediation programmes. At the time they seemed to be invaluable tools to support information security or business continuity planning; but they fell into disuse because there was no obvious person or incentive to maintain them.

Mature IT organizations generally have an existing, enterprise-wide network of IT managers responsible for maintaining business application portfolios. This is the logical level, therefore, at which to collect and maintain information regarding the priority or status of security requirements and controls. There are often limitations, however, in the scope for populating existing systems or databases used for IT applications portfolio management with security information. In most cases, a separate database or spreadsheet will need to be established initially. But, ideally, such a system should be integrated into the application portfolio management process in order to establish a capability for its longer-term maintenance.

5.5 Conducting a risk assessment

5.5.1 The need to assess risk

Any change in the sourcing of an essential business service will have a significant impact on business and security risk profiles. Some risks will be unchanged in probability or impact, but many will be different, if only because of changes in infrastructure, systems, operational managers or locations. There will also be a range of new risks introduced, such as the possibility of the outsourcer going bankrupt.

All risks will need to be carefully identified, assessed and either accepted, or mitigated through an appropriate set of actions. For many organizations outsourcing will result in a potential reduction in some forms of risk. For example, there might be lower risks of failures in service delivery through improved skills, processes and technologies. But these gains will also be accompanied by a number of potential downside risks, through, for example, a major loss of visibility and direct control.

ISO/IEC 27036 recommends that the customer organization should implement a security risk management approach to address all aspects of the security risks to be managed, in order to ensure a consistent quality of service. The recommended approach is based on BS ISO/IEC 27005, *Information technology – Security techniques – Information security risk management*, the International Standard for information security risk assessment, and it includes the following steps:

- identification of the relevant risks and vulnerabilities, their likelihood and impact on the acquirer's service to be outsourced;
- identification of the relevant stakeholders, their concerns, and possible reactions to adverse events;
- assessment of the identified risks;
- identification of the existing or planned mitigations for each risk;
- assessment of the residual (untreated) risk based on the reduced impact and/or likelihood that result from mitigation.

The outcomes from the risk assessment should support the acquirer in determining the level of acceptable security risks and deciding if this level is acceptable or not.

The standard recommends that any initial decision to outsource should be reconsidered when the security risks are high and cannot be effectively reduced, or when the security controls are assessed to be inadequate. The standard also recommends that a cost–benefit analysis should be performed to determine the net benefit of outsourcing a service, taking into account

- the cost of the outsourcing agreement,
- the cost of mitigating the associated risks,
- the residual (untreated or accepted) risks, and
- the expected benefits that will be realized through the outsourcing agreement.

Establishing detailed costs at the planning stage, however, is difficult if not impossible prior to a comprehensive review by the outsourcer of the client's requirements and the submission of a proposal. The overall cost of the outsourcing will generally depend on vendor service *prices* rather than existing customer *costs*, and precise figures will not be known until after the proposals are submitted by the vendors bidding for the contract.

5.5.2 Factors that impact risk assessment

Risk management is more of a blunt instrument than an exact science. It should be regarded, primarily, as a decision-support tool rather a decision-making technique. Risk assessment helps to prioritize action and to inform and justify decision-making. Major business decisions, however, are always best when based on the full, rich, available detail of the situation under consideration, rather than on the basis of a concise, abbreviated description of a risk and a broad set of ratings.

Conducting a risk assessment might sound like a relatively straightforward process. But it is far from easy, because of a number of factors which serve to blur or complicate matters. These factors need to be addressed in drawing up a suitable method of risk assessment.

The first factor is that many people are unfamiliar with or have varying ideas of what 'risk' means in a business context. If you ask a group of business managers to produce a list of risks, you'll probably get a mixture of subject areas such as 'compliance', and issues or requirements such as 'budget cuts', as well as actual risks such as 'data breaches'. And risks are not just negative factors. They are specific events with a probability and an impact. Such events can include positive outcomes, such as an increase in revenue or profit, but this is generally unlikely when we're considering *security* risks. Many forms of business and financial risk have an upside, but security risks are events that we aim to avoid. The key learning point, however, is the need to ensure that the people responsible for identifying and assessing the risks are educated in what is meant by a risk. This topic is addressed in the next section.

The second factor is that our perception of risks tends to be a relative rather than an absolute assessment. Each of us has widely varying attitudes to risk, shaped by factors such as our age, gender, personality, lifestyle, religion, culture, role, logical ability, objectives and personal experience. The size of a risk is, to a large extent, in the eye of the beholder. For many managers, their assessment of a risk will be heavily influenced by its perceived impact on current scorecards and bonus-related targets. For this reason, it is best to assess risks as part of a team exercise.

The third factor is that it is very hard for people to assess any new thing without comparing and contrasting it against something with which they are already familiar. This is a natural psychological phenomenon. It means that when we consider risks, we tend to judge them by comparing their relative probability or impact against risks which we've previously assessed or experienced. That's why it's much better to ask business managers to rank, rather than quantify, risks.

The fourth factor is that, for many risks, we simply don't have the necessary facts or insight to judge them properly. Managers cannot be expected to pinpoint the precise likelihood and impact of new risks, or the effectiveness of countermeasures for any incident that's outside of their experience. For this reason, it's useful to seek some form of external input when identifying and assessing outsourcing risks, preferably from a colleague or a consultant who has been through a similar exercise before.

The fifth factor is the wide potential variation in the scope of identified risks. Some managers tend to identify rather general risk descriptions, such as 'a major data breach'. Others prefer to single out more specific risk descriptions, such as 'the loss of a laptop containing unencrypted customer credit card details'. In fact, there is no perfect scope, as there are numerous interpretations of the former and an infinite number of the latter. Brainstorming sessions will generate examples of both types of risk. A degree of standardization before the session, or some normalization after the event, will therefore be required to refine the results.

The sixth factor is that risks can be looked at from two perspectives: either gross or net of controls. Most managers think in terms of net risks: the ones that remain after existing countermeasures have been applied. But many professional risk managers also consider gross risks: the ones that would exist if no countermeasures were in place. Net risks are much easier to comprehend and assess, but gross risks can provide an indication of what might happen if someone ignored or evaded the established controls. Clear definitions and guidance on what constitutes a risk are required.

BS ISO 31000, *Risk management – Principles and guidelines* also provides a useful reference for the implementation of risk management. This standard is intended to provide best practice structure and guidance to all operations concerned with risk management, including the design, implementation and maintenance of risk management processes. It is broader in scope than BS ISO/IEC 27005, mentioned earlier, which focuses primarily on information security.

5.5.3 What constitutes a risk?

Given that risks are such difficult, slippery items to identify and assess, it invites the question as to precisely how we should define them. This is certainly not a new problem, though the science is surprisingly immature. There are even standards such as PD ISO/IEC Guide 73, *Risk Management – Vocabulary – Guidelines for use in standards*, which sets out the vocabulary to be used in risk management, though most of these concepts are now well-established and understood. In business today, risks are generally regarded as a combination of the probability of a damaging event, whether deliberate or accidental, and the resulting business impact.

This is a simple approach, but a pragmatic one. We could, in fact, further subdivide the risk into several factors, such as the value or attractiveness of the asset at risk, the size of the threats, or the vulnerability of the organization to such threats. But such an analysis would add little value to what is at best a rough estimate, and it would serve to further complicate the assessment.

The key concept behind risk management is that we have a set of corporate assets of value to the organization which might be vulnerable to specific threats, but are safeguarded by controls or countermeasures which prevent or mitigate the business impact of the risk occurring. Probabilities of a risk, or damaging event, tend to measure in terms of a fraction from zero to one, or a percentage, based on the probability of occurrence over a period of time, typically a year. If a risk is assigned a probability of one, or 100%, this means it's certain to happen in the chosen timescale.

The scale for measuring business impact value can be anything that is convenient for the operation of the risk management process, such as a simple range of one to five. What counts is not the absolute value of the calculations, though this is useful for business cases, but their relative rankings which enable prioritization of remedial actions. That is essentially the language of risk management. Managers should not need a technologist or an International

Standard to grasp the basics, though an experienced practitioner can help to safely navigate them around the many pitfalls.

Risk management is a simple process that aims to identify, assess and prioritize risks for remedial action. Individual risks are considered and, if significant, entered in a risk register, which ranks them and presents them in the form of a league table, in order of priority, based on a combination of their likelihood and business impact.

5.5.4 Identifying and assessing risks

Risks can be identified in a number of ways: from a consideration of threats to a particular asset, such as a data centre; by listing out a set of risks associated with a project (which should be a standard project management output); or by conducting a walk-through of a business value chain and identifying the various hazards that might impact its successful execution. An alternative method could be to simply carry out a free-form brainstorming session for a particular purpose or scenario such as, in this case, outsourcing.

Conducting a risk identification and assessment exercise for a major initiative is best done as a team effort with a group of senior-level business stakeholders, perhaps accompanied by a range of specialists selected from functions such as legal, procurement, finance, human resources, internal audit, IT and security. As mentioned above, it's better to assess risks as a team exercise, both to exploit the resultant sharing of knowledge and to reduce the impact of any cognitive bias in assessments.

Checklists of common risks facing organizations can be useful to help identify potential risks, by prompting ideas and discussion and acting as a check for obvious omissions. Free-form brainstorming is also useful, as it helps to identify risks not previously encountered, which might be unique to this initiative. Security risks can be identified as a separate exercise or as part of a more general assessment of business risks. But a very general assessment of risks is likely to be too broad to identify many of the more specialist security risks.

For ease of analysis, risks are most easily captured and ranked using a simple two-by-two chart, which makes it easy to capture, agree and position a range of risks relative to each other. An example is shown in Figure 3.

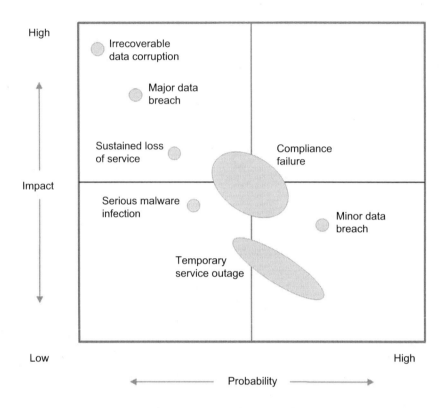

Figure 3 – Example of a chart used for identifying and ranking the relative impact of risks

Figure 3 is based on the two major dimensions of risks: probability and business impact. The rankings from 'high' to 'low' in each dimension are relatively easy to agree in practice, avoiding the need for quantification, which is much more complex to assess and agree. Subsequent research can be done to confirm details and generally fine-tune the results.

Checklists and prompts can also be used to focus discussions. There are many techniques to structure such exercises, based for example on lists of threats or categories of security controls. Perhaps the most useful example is to consider risks within the well-known 'PESTLE' categories: Political, Economic, Socio-cultural, Technological, Legal and Environmental.

5.5.5 Managing the risks

Once an agreed set of risks have been identified and assessed, it will be necessary to quantify them, as realistically as possible, based on their likelihood and business impact. This process will generate a risk register which can be easily updated and added to with new information on actions, responsibilities and progress. Figure 4 shows a typical extract from a risk register.

Items to consider including in a risk register are

- the name and description of the risk,
- the stakeholder responsible,
- the relative size of the risk in terms of impact and probability,
- the risk appetite, such as tolerate or fix,
- compensating controls in place, and
- remedial actions, with responsibilities and completion dates.

A common problem when compiling risk registers is that managers at different levels in an organization will tend to rank or qualify business impacts quite differently. A loss of a million dollars will seem much more significant to a junior manager than it will to a divisional director. On the other hand, the divisional director might also need to consider the broader impact of a loss being aggregated across several business units.

The identified risks can be addressed in a variety of ways: by avoiding them, reducing their severity, transferring them to someone else, or by simply keeping your fingers crossed and accepting them. In practice we tend to use a combination of these options.

Avoiding the risk is generally the most satisfactory option, but it's also likely to prove to be the most expensive. It means scaling back the ambitions of the initiative, or applying additional countermeasures, such as enhanced supervision or monitoring.

Reducing the severity of the risk can be done in a number of ways, for example through better fallback arrangements or improved incident response processes and contingency plans.

Transferring the risk through some form of hedging or insurance can also be considered, but the options and scenarios in which this can be used are very limited.

Ref	Description of risk	Business impact			Risk score	Risk treatment		
		Extent of impact	Est. value	Probability		Risk owner	Action	Date
01	Compliance failure through oversight in contract	Penalty fine, reputation damage, cost of remedial action	$1 m	Med/High		D. Lacey	Gap analysis	End June 2010

Figure 4 – Example of a risk register

Accepting the risk presents a further risk in itself, as it points the finger as to where accountability might lie for any consequential impact.

5.6 Reviewing policies and standards

5.6.1 An opportunity to take stock

The planning and preparation stage is also an ideal time to review security policies and standards. Many might be incomplete or out of date, as security needs are constantly evolving to meet emerging threats or respond to new vulnerabilities or new compliance requirements. Delays in the implementation of policies and standards are a further concern.

Policies and standards should be forward-looking, but consistent with actual practice. As soon as the procurement commences, potential bidders will ask to examine customer policies, architectures and standards. The level of inspection and cooperation will become progressively broader and deeper as the commercial process progresses. Customers need to be well prepared for such transparency, by ensuring that all relevant internal documentation is current, relevant and in a fit state to be presented to an outside party.

Setting a higher security standard than can be readily achieved will create a major inconsistency. Potential contractors will carry out due diligence prior to presenting a proposal, and their bids will reflect the level of security practised, rather than the one desired. Gaps in compliance of legacy systems should ideally be identified and addressed before the contract is signed to avoid expensive post-contract changes. Constraints on budget, manpower and time, however, will limit the opportunity for immediate changes. It will be necessary therefore to negotiate an appropriate longer-term arrangement for bringing non-compliant legacy systems into line with current policies and standards.

Policies and standards can be written and presented in a number of ways. Guidance can be prescriptive, insisting that something must be done in one particular way and no other. Or it can be flexible, enabling the recipient to interpret it to suit local circumstances. Guidance can also be very detailed, with lengthy accounts of what should be done, or it can be reduced down to a smaller number of high-level guiding principles or control objectives.

Some organizations have distinctive 'house styles' for policies and standards, but in many cases it is generally left to the author of the document to select the title and then decide the length of the guidance and the choice of words. At the planning stage for an outsourcing programme it is important to try to ensure that formal policies and standards are consistent, realistic and appropriately presented. Each document should therefore be individually reviewed, and subject to document control to enable changes to be tracked and review dates monitored.

The choice of title, length and phrasing of a document influence its tone and interpretation. In the case of a dispute, these choices might also have legal consequences. Words such as 'must', 'may', 'can', 'should' or 'shall' convey different meanings regarding the degree of compulsion or adaptability implied. These words should be clearly defined and not used interchangeably. Common interpretations for a policy or standard would be that the word 'should' expresses a recommendation; the word 'may' expresses permissibility; and the word 'can' expresses possibility.

Deciding the most appropriate style depends on whether a prescriptive or flexible approach is desired. Each has advantages. The former approach might be more appropriate for a short-term development contract, for example, with an offshore contractor, where communications need to be absolutely clear and the rules need to be precisely specified. On the other hand, a lighter touch might be more appropriate for a longer-term partnership with a large, sophisticated outsourcer, where a greater degree of empowerment and flexibility is required to take advantage of the skills and practices available, as well as to cater for future changes.

There are two main dimensions in framing security guidance: level of detail and degree of prescription. Figure 5 illustrates four possible options for a security policy or standard: guiding principles, big rules, code of practice or conformance standard.

Big rules are mandatory, high-level, governance requirements that must be obeyed, but the detail of the implementation is left to the recipient.

Guiding principles are more subtle: a set of design guidelines, for example, that shape the execution of the activities within scope.

A **code of practice** is a form of standard that's designed to allow a degree of flexibility in local interpretation. A good example of that is BS ISO/IEC 27002,

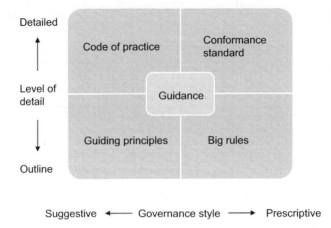

Figure 5 – Options for presenting security guidance

Information technology – Security techniques – Code of practice for information security management, which is intended to be adaptable to a range of organizations with widely different environments and risk profiles.

This type of standard is quite different in tone, style and wording from a more prescriptive **conformance standard** that might, for example, be needed to define a specific communications protocol.

A good information security framework will exploit all of these options. There is nothing inconsistent in combining these requirements, as long as we avoid mixing the choice of words within the same guideline. Prescriptive guidelines are generally more appropriate for expressing requirements for technical controls, and codes of practice for management processes. But there are no hard and fast rules.

For longer-term ease of maintenance – an important consideration for policies and standards – it pays to design an efficient structure, with volatile items of information, such as names of people, locations and technologies, in separate documents or annexes from more general information such as control objectives and design principles. Long-lasting content should not be mixed with fast-changing text, as this will make future maintenance difficult and new document releases harder to review.

5.6.2 Security policies

Most organizations set out to maintain a simple, clear security policy for their employees. In practice, however, they tend to accumulate a growing portfolio of security policies as new technologies or issues come to light, each demanding a clear statement of corporate policy. Examples of these might be the introduction in recent years of laptop encryption, mobile working or social networking.

Key subject areas that might justify a dedicated security policy include the following. These are areas requiring specific rules and detailed advice which cannot be conveyed in a more general policy document:

- information security classification;
- third-party access to corporate systems;
- security incident management;
- penetration testing;
- vulnerability management;
- security of wireless networks;
- mobile working;
- use of Web 2.0 technologies and social networking;
- use of cryptography and key management.

Many areas of security policy, such as basic principles, general accountabilities and classification labels, are relatively long-lasting. Other areas, such as references to standards, approval processes and incident reporting points are generally more volatile, requiring periodic review and updating. The planning process for a major outsourcing programme provides a useful opportunity for an organization to overhaul its existing security policies, rationalize their structure and content, and bring them up to date.

5.6.3 Security architecture

Every organization needs a set of architectures to manage its business processes, information systems and, increasingly, its security. Architectures are essential to develop and maintain enterprise systems, for example. Complex systems require some form of structure to help set out the designer's thoughts, communicate the specification, and provide an efficient means of maintenance. In the absence of a clearly defined, modular structure it is extremely difficult to apply major changes.

Security architectures, however, are different from the type of architecture we use to design business processes or construct information systems. They tend to be selective, unbalanced and incomplete, as they are intended primarily to identify control requirements and security technology choices, which are neither static nor pervasive. Security requirements are volatile and evolving, responding to changes in risk profiles, compliance requirements and security incidents.

Security architectures can be developed at various levels, addressing high-level compliance requirements, mid-level control objectives, or low-level technology choices. The most important concept is to recognize that security architectures are a means to an end, and it is the end that is most important. From a customer perspective, that end is the need to convey key design decisions regarding security requirements, in particular those that cannot be derived from a policy or set of standards.

5.6.4 Security standards

There are several international or British standards that are useful to consider when reviewing corporate standards, and these are briefly described below. These standards are useful reference documents when drawing up contracts or specifications for new systems and services, as well as when evaluating responses from potential outsourcers. Some of these standards focus on security requirements, some are more general governance or service management standards, and others are specialist ones that address specific subject areas such as security of payment card data, business continuity, risk management, and even how to manage security in the supply chain.

When contemplating a move from an in-house to an external source of supply, it's more efficient and appropriate to adopt public standards as far as possible, rather than attempt to impose in-house standards on suppliers who will be striving to achieve economies of scale and consistency of services for a wide range of customers. Many of the standards described below have a degree of duplication and overlap. They can also be relatively expensive to purchase, especially for a large internal readership, so it's important to understand when and how to use them.

Each standard has its own merits, and its value to an organization will depend on the scope, context and purpose for which it will be used. Most of the differences in structure and coverage between the standards are the result of the different perspectives of the organizations or standards committees responsible for their development.

Standards are best applied within the context in which they were developed, though they can also serve as useful background information and checklists when drawing up contract schedules. Some are excellent control specifications; others are more suitable as a basis for structuring service management requirements or designing new governance processes. Some are well established; others relatively new and not yet widely adopted.

Attempts have been made from time to time to combine or cross-reference the most popular standards. The results of such exercises can be useful for reference purposes, but the length and complexity of the material generated is too unwieldy to be useful for day-to-day business purposes.

BS ISO/IEC 27002 (Information security)

Many security standards have been developed over the years, but few have stood the test of time as well as the International Standard BS ISO/IEC 27002, *Information technology – Security techniques – Code of practice for information security management*, which is based on a BSI document originally published in 1993. As a code of practice, no individual elements of the standard are mandatory. Suitable information security controls can be selected by the organization on the basis of a risk assessment to address particular control objectives. This standard addresses the following areas:

- security policy;
- organization of information security;
- asset management;
- human resources security;
- physical and environmental security;
- communications and operations management;
- access control;
- information systems acquisition, development and maintenance;
- information security incident management;
- business continuity management;
- regulatory compliance.

I have to admit to a marked preference for this standard, as well as a unique insight into its development, as I drafted most of the original content on which it was based during my time in the Royal Dutch/Shell Group. There are three main reasons why this standard has been so successful.

Firstly, it was a management standard drawn up by experienced industry practitioners, rather than academic, vendor or standards specialists. The core material was also based on established industry security practices, rather than a set of theoretical security requirements.

Secondly, it was developed with professional advice from a standards authority, which distinguishes it from standards such as the Payment Card Industry Data Security Standard, which were developed without detailed consideration of the practical issues associated with implementation, certification and long-term maintenance.

And, thirdly, it has continued to evolve with professional oversight from many experienced practitioners and subject matter experts. This standard offers many advantages to any organization intending to outsource. It is internationally recognized, and it offers the powerful benefit of a formal accredited certification process, an essential governance process in order to 'close the loop' and ensure that commitments to the adoption of the controls in the standard are matched by their actual implementation.

An accompanying standard, BS ISO/IEC 27001, *Information technology – Security techniques – Information security management systems – Requirements* is a specification for an information security management system (ISMS). This standard is not a code of practice with advice on countermeasures, but it is a certifiable standard within the suite of information security standards. Certification is granted through an accredited certification body, which aims to ensure that a consistent methodology and a minimum level of experience and skills are applied to the audit process.

These two standards are part of the BS ISO/IEC 27000 series, a broader, emerging family of standards on information security techniques and management systems. Future standards under development in this series include an ISMS implementation guide. These standards were primarily designed for organizations that mostly manage their own in-house IT operations. They address third-party outsourced operations, but largely as an exception rather than a rule.

Outsourcing, however, demands a greater focus on the management of the interface between the customer and the outsourcer. The BS ISO/IEC 27000

---

series of standards addresses the *content* of what needs to be implemented, but it might not convey the optimum balance and emphasis for what needs to be individually achieved by each party in an outsourced relationship. These standards should be applied within the context of the outsourcing programme, and the envisaged division of accountabilities between customer and supplier.

The Payment Card Industry Data Security Standard

Any organization that processes customer credit card data will also need to consider the implications of the Payment Card Industry Data Security Standard (PCI DSS), an internationally recognized information security standard created to prevent payment card fraud through a specified set of controls to safeguard customer payment card data. The standard applies to all retail organizations that hold, process, or pass cardholder information from any card branded with the logo of one of the major card brands. Compliance is mandatory and must be validated annually through a self-assessment questionnaire for companies handling relatively small volumes of payment card transactions, or by an independent, qualified security assessor for organizations handling large volumes of transactions.

The PCI DSS is a set of principles and prescriptive control requirements for safeguarding cardholder data. The structure is different from BS ISO/IEC 27002, based on 12 control requirements in six categories of control objective.[5]

1) Build and maintain a secure network
- Install and maintain a firewall configuration to protect cardholder data.
- Do not use vendor-supplied defaults for system passwords and other security parameters.

2) Protect cardholder data
- Protect stored cardholder data.
- Encrypt transmission of cardholder data across open, public networks.

3) Maintain a vulnerability management programme
- Use and regularly update anti-virus software.
- Develop and maintain secure systems and applications.

---

[5] Behind these headings are a large number of individual, prescriptive requirements. At the time of writing this book, PCI DSS included 247 specific requirements within these 12 control headings.

4) Implement strong access control measures
- Restrict access to cardholder data by business need-to-know.
- Assign a unique ID to each person with computer access.
- Restrict physical access to cardholder data.

5) Regularly monitor and test networks
- Track and monitor all access to network resources and cardholder data.
- Regularly test security systems and processes.

6) Maintain an information security policy
- Maintain a policy that addresses information security.

The targets of the PCI DSS standard extend beyond the traditional scope of many information security managers, encompassing remote front-office retail operations as well as call centres, which are services that are prime business targets for outsourcing and offshoring.

Control Objectives for Information and related Technology

Control Objectives for Information and related Technology (COBIT) is a set of best practice controls for IT management created by the Information Systems Audit and Control Association and the IT Governance Institute in 1996, a few years after the publication of BS 7799, *Information security management systems – Guidelines for information security risk management*, the standard that formed the basis of BS ISO/IEC 27002. COBIT covers four domains: Plan and organize; Acquire and implement; Deliver and support; and Monitor and evaluate. It has a broader scope than BS ISO/IEC 27002, as it addresses IT governance rather than information security.

These two standards are not intended to compete with each other, and are partly complementary, but there is considerable overlap between them. BS ISO/IEC 27002 has stronger security content, but COBIT has broader scope for IT governance and service management. In fact, COBIT is one of several standards that can be used to help establish a more disciplined and standardized IT management framework.

Other important frameworks include the Information Technology Infrastructure Library (ITIL) and BS ISO/IEC 20000, *Information technology – Service management*. These standards work very well with traditional, well-defined processes and services, such as enterprise resource management systems, but they can be rigid and bureaucratic for more innovative environments, such as the growing networks that support more dynamic developments based on emerging Web 2.0 technologies.

Information Technology Infrastructure Library (ITIL)

The Information Technology Infrastructure Library (ITIL) is a set of concepts and practices for managing IT services, developed originally by the UK Office of Government Commerce and currently used by thousands of organizations across the world. It covers both development and operational processes and provides detailed descriptions of common IT practices, as well as checklists, tasks and procedures that organizations can tailor to suit their individual needs.

ITIL is a well-established and widely used framework of best practices for IT service management, supported by books, training courses and professional qualifications. It focuses on the provision of IT services, as well as the environmental facilities required to support them. Among other things, it serves as a useful benchmark for the professional management of IT services. ITIL has a similar scope but a different perspective from COBIT, as it focuses primarily on processes rather than control objectives. ITIL is therefore more useful and relevant for IT managers defining service requirements, rather than security managers and auditors defining business controls requirements.

The processes set out in ITIL are intended to support and be supported by other International Standards for IT service management, including BS ISO/IEC 20000. In fact, the ITIL service support and delivery volumes are generally equivalent to the scope of BS ISO/IEC 20000, though there are some differences in detail, for example in the definition of assets and in the overall scope of the standards (ITIL is broader). Organizations cannot achieve formal certification under ITIL, but they can seek certification under BS ISO/IEC 20000.

A key requirement under ITIL is that the customer documents a business information security policy to define the high-level security requirements that IT services and service management processes will be required need to meet. This document can either be produced as a discrete, self-contained recapitulation of the 'big rules', or as a cross-reference to statements in other existing high-level policy documentation. Either way, it must be aligned with the information security management system. The business information security policy is the starting point for mapping customer security requirements onto ITIL documentation.

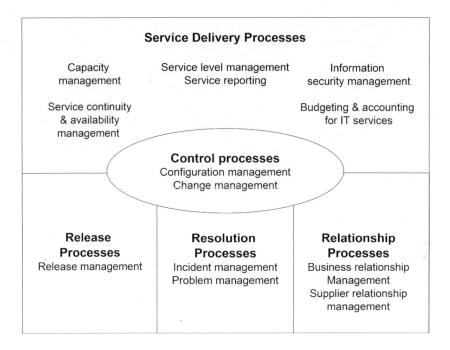

Figure 6 – IT service management processes

ITIL focuses on assets, changes, configurations, incidents and reporting. It covers the introduction of new IT capabilities and services into the operational environment, but provides less detail on how these are developed. An ITIL compliant management process might not embody all aspects of information security. Further models or guidelines might be necessary to cover requirements associated with systems development, acquisition and integration.

BS ISO/IEC 20000, Information technology – Service management

The BS ISO/IEC 20000 series of standards is designed for IT service providers and aims to help them enhance the quality of services delivered to customers, whether internal and external. Like ITIL, these standards are structured around best practices in *processes*, and are intended to be independent of organizational form, size or functional structure. Figure 6 illustrates the structure and range of processes defined by BS ISO/IEC 20000.

Planning and preparation

The BS ISO/IEC 20000 series of standards is designed to apply to both large and small service providers. It comprises three standards.

Part 1 is a specification that defines the requirements for service providers to deliver managed services. This can be used by customers going out to tender for services, and it can help to encourage a consistent approach by a range of different service providers operating across a supply chain, as might be provided by a consortium of outsourcing suppliers. This standard also promotes the adoption of an integrated process approach to the delivery of managed services. Establishing such an integrated approach to service management processes enables tighter control, greater efficiency and broader opportunities for improvement.

Part 2 of BS ISO/IEC 20000 is a code of practice, in common with the pattern of BS ISO/IEC 27000, and Part 3 provides further guidance on scope definition and applicability. These standards cover a broader range of subjects than just security, but they provide a framework for general service management that helps enable the ownership of key security activities and controls to be more formally defined and embedded.

BS ISO 28000, Specification for security management systems for the supply chain

This series of standards defines the requirements for a *physical* security management system, addressing those aspects that are critical to the security assurance of a business supply chain. It is different in focus and scope from the BS ISO/IEC 27000 series, but newer and less established. The BS ISO 28000 series of standard has been designed primarily for logistics companies and organizations that manage supply chain operations.

The standard is useful for companies that need to comply with European Union regulations for supply chain security to satisfy customs and border protection initiatives. BS ISO 28000 employs a pragmatic approach to security, in which controls are applied according to risk levels identified in the supply chain. This standard is designed to be applicable to all sizes and types of organization, from small enterprises to large global enterprises operating in a range of sectors, including manufacturing, service, storage or transportation, at any stage of the production or supply chain. The series includes a number of publications:

- BS ISO 28001, *Security management systems for the supply chain – Best practices for implementing supply chain security, assessments and plans – Requirements and guidance;*
- BS ISO 28003, *Security management systems for the supply chain – Requirements for bodies providing audit and certification of supply chain security management systems;*
- BS ISO 28004, *Security management systems for the supply chain – Guidelines for the implementation of ISO 28000.*

In common with BS ISO/IEC 27001 and BS ISO/IEC 20000, BS ISO 28000 is a certifiable standard. It is also designed to be compatible with the BS EN ISO 9001, *Quality Management Systems Requirements* and BS EN ISO 14001, *Environmental Management Systems* standards, enabling a more integrated and consistent approach to be taken to the management of risks across the supply chain, especially for logistics companies or other organizations where quality, physical and environment requirements are also important business issues. This standard will also be a useful reference for organizations already operating these compatible standards, or those who might wish to integrate corporate policies and governance processes for security, quality and environmental management.

BS ISO 31000 (Risk management)

A relatively new International Standard, BS ISO 31000: *Risk management – Principles and guidelines* is designed to help organizations of all types and sizes to manage risk effectively. It sets out principles, a framework and a process for managing any form of risk in a transparent, systematic and credible manner, within any scope or context. ISO has also published PD ISO/IEC Guide 73, *Risk management – Vocabulary – Guidelines for use in standards*, which complements BS ISO 31000 by providing a collection of terms and definitions relating to the management of risk. There are many sources of freely available guidance on how to go about risk management, but BS ISO 31000 is one of the few *de jure* standards in the field.

BS 25999 (Business continuity)

Ensuring continued business operations in the event of a disruption, whether due to a major disaster or minor incident, is a fundamental requirement for all organizations. BS 25999, a British Standard for business continuity management, has been developed to help businesses to minimize the risk and impact of such disruptions.

This standard has been developed by a group of international experts representing a cross-section of industry and government sectors to establish the process, principles and terminology of business continuity management. It contains a comprehensive set of requirements based on best industry practice, covering the complete business continuity planning lifecycle. The standard is in two parts:

- *Part 1: Code of Practice* provides best-practice recommendations. It is essentially a guidance document;
- *Part 2: Specification* provides the requirements for a business continuity management system. This is the part of the standard that can be used to demonstrate compliance via an auditing and certification process.

Information security standards such as BS ISO/IEC 27002 include a chapter on business continuity, but BS 25999 is broader in scope, though consistent in approach.

PAS 99 (Integrated management system)

PAS 99, *Specification of common management system requirements as a framework for integration*, is an integrated management system requirements specification based on the six common requirements of ISO Guide 72 (a standard for writing management system standards). The prefix 'PAS' indicates a Publicly Available Specification, which is a step towards a British Standard, though it does not guarantee that such a standard will eventually be published. It was developed to align management processes and procedures into a single holistic structure that might enable organizations to run their operations more effectively.

This initiative reflects a general trend towards convergence in governance functions, which, among other things, helps to streamline management overheads and reduce senior executive headcount. Integrated management is suitable for any organization, regardless of size or sector, looking to integrate two or more of their management systems into one cohesive system with a holistic set of documentation, policies, procedures and processes. A typical integrated management system might include:

- BS EN ISO 9001, *Quality management systems*;
- BS EN ISO 14001, *Environmental management systems*;

- BS OHSAS 18001, *Occupational health and safety management systems*;
- BS ISO/IEC 27001, *Information technology – Security techniques*;
- BS EN ISO 22000, *Food safety management systems*;
- BS ISO/IEC 20000, *Information technology – Service management*.

This list is not intended to be finite, and the range of standards incorporated into the integrated management system can vary. PAS 99 is a Publicly Available Specification of common requirements for management systems that can be used as a framework for an integrated management system. It is intended to encourage organizations with more than one management system to view PAS 99 as the opportunity to achieve a single holistic management system, which will enable them to more effectively run their operations.

PAS 99 takes account of the six common requirements for management systems standards outlined in ISO Guide 72. It follows the 'Plan, Do, Check, Act' approach of all the major management systems requirements standards. These six common requirements are

1) policy,
2) planning,
3) implementation and operation,
4) performance assessment,
5) improvement, and
6) management review.

PAS 99 provides a useful template for designing, specifying or evaluating management system processes and requirements. In the context of outsourcing, PAS 99 can serve as a useful vehicle for structuring, specifying and converging governance processes and contractual requirements satisfying a range of different functional requirements for a single outsourcer.

BS ISO/IEC 38500 (IT Governance)

BS ISO/IEC 38500, *Corporate governance of information technology* is a relatively recent standard that provides guiding principles for directors of organizations, including owners, board members, directors, partners and senior executives, on the effective, efficient, and acceptable use of IT within their organization. It applies to the governance of management processes and decisions relating to the information and communication services used by an organization.

The framework comprises definitions, principles and a model. It sets out six principles for good corporate governance of IT:

1) responsibility;
2) strategy;
3) acquisition;
4) performance;
5) conformance;
6) human behaviour.

Readers will note that this is a different structure from that adopted by other standards that address IT service management, but the focus is different, aiming at a more senior customer audience. In the context of an outsourcing initiative, it can serve as a useful basis for informing senior management and IT strategy committees on the roles and principles that apply to the corporate governance of IT within and outside of their organization.

5.7 Learning points from this chapter

This chapter has explored the many areas of planning and preparation required prior to outsourcing. Key learning points to note can be summarized as follows.

▶ Good planning and preparation is a vital step in outsourcing and offshoring. It is the critical point to identify major security risks and requirements, which will inform management of security and compliance issues, and identify overheads that might not have been considered in the business case.

▶ Security, compliance and risk considerations need to be addressed at all stages of the outsourcing lifecycle, from conception to termination. It is harder and more expensive to address these issues the later they are identified. Changes requested after outsourcing are likely to prove very expensive. The business case for outsourcing might also become less attractive as planning proceeds and overlooked costs come to light, resulting in political pressure to move quickly and freeze specifications.

▶ Key decision points requiring security input are
  • at the outset when a decision is made to proceed,
  • at the definition stage when the scope of the outsourcing is determined,
  • during the planning and selection stage when proposals are invited,

- when developing and negotiating the contract,
- when implementing the new arrangements, and
- when considering future changes.

▶ The starting point is to estimate likely costs, benefits and risks. The next step is to identify and classify sensitive, critical or valuable assets warranting special attention. Risk assessments will need to be conducted to identify and assess the most significant security risks. Security policies, architecture and standards will also need to be reviewed to ensure they are current and appropriate.

▶ The major constraint in achieving all of this is the limited time and resources available. Modern 'discovery' technologies can help to identify corporate assets and to map data flows. But prioritization is the key, based on the sensitivity and importance of assets and the relative size of the identified risks.

▶ Security classifications are a powerful tool, both for highlighting assets requiring priority attention and simplifying decision processes. Complex systems should be avoided. Two or three labels are more than enough for most people to handle. One problem to watch for is that similar labels can have different interpretations across a supply chain.

▶ Sensitive, critical and valuable data can be identified by drawing up categories, or asking open questions such as 'What are the crown jewels of the organization?' Registers of classified assets are best organized by business application portfolio and maintained by portfolio managers.

▶ Risk management is a blunt instrument rather than an exact science. It is a decision-support tool rather than a decision-making technique. Risk assessment helps prioritize action and inform and justify decisions. Major business decisions should be made using all available information, rather than on a narrow set of ratings.

▶ Conducting a risk assessment can be difficult as there will be many gaps in the knowledge required, and people's perception of risks can be influenced by their personality and experience. It is easier to rank rather than quantify risks. Risks can be general or specific, and gross or net of existing controls. BS ISO/IEC 31000, *Risk management – Principles and guidelines* provides a useful, common reference for risk management.

▶ Risks can be identified from a consideration of threats to assets, risks to projects, or hazards to business value chains. Risk assessment is best done as a team effort with business stakeholders and selected functional specialists. Risks can be addressed in a variety of ways: by avoiding them, reducing their severity, transferring them to someone else, or accepting them. A combination of these options is generally required in practice.

▶ The planning stage is a good time to review security policies and standards. Many will be incomplete or out of date, as security needs are constantly evolving. Documentation should be forward-looking, but must be consistent with actual practice. Guidance can be detailed and prescriptive or based on high-level control objectives, but it must be consistent, realistic and appropriately presented.

▶ It is better to adopt public standards as far as possible, rather than impose in-house standards on suppliers, who might be aiming to deliver consistent services for a range of customers. Standards can be useful as a specification, or as a basis for structuring service requirements, or when designing governance processes. Popular security and IT management standards include BS ISO/IEC 27002, *Information technology – Security techniques – Code of practice for information security management*, COBIT and ITIL. A growing range of more specialist standards are also available and these are outlined in this chapter.

6 Selecting a supplier

6.1 Key questions to consider

When considering supplier selection, it's useful to start by considering the following questions, as they will help to identify the tasks that will need to be carried out before and during the selection process.

- How will security considerations be inputted to the overall supplier selection process?
- How will candidate suppliers be provided with information to help them frame their proposals, and what information will they need?
- How will the customer gain confidence in a potential supplier's security capabilities?
- On what basis will the final selection decision be made?

6.2 The selection process

The formal selection process generally begins with a 'request for proposal' (RFP), prepared by the customer and issued to a range of potential suppliers. The RFP should clearly set out the objectives, requirements and expectations for the services in scope. It should include details of all relevant security policies, standards and control requirements, as well as the security information to be provided in the proposals and the security criteria for judging the suitability of the potential contractors' formal submissions.

The selection process also requires a series of security checks to be made on the reliability and capability of the short listed bidders. This type of process is usually referred to as due diligence, and is necessary to protect the interests of the customer organization. At the same time, the potential vendors will also be carrying out their own process of due diligence to ensure that they fully understand the customer requirements, as well as the associated costs of meeting them.

Documents outlining key policies, architectures, standards and processes will need to be made available through some form of physical or online 'team room' (or 'data room'). Traditionally, suppliers have been allowed supervised access to a physical team room, at set dates and times, to study information to help them frame their bids. Increasingly, the team room is becoming an online rather than a physical space, due to the volume of documentation it needs to accommodate and the diverse, remote access needs that arise in a modern selection process.

Constructing a secure electronic team room is a minor security project in its own right, not just because of the sensitivity of the information, but also to ensure that the candidate suppliers do not become aware of each others' identities. Care is needed in the design and implementation process to ensure, for example, that mailing lists for new documents being added do not disclose the identities of individual recipients to other users.

The documents provided in the team room will need to be genuine, realistic and up-to-date if the bidders are to make realistic estimates of the costs of delivering compliant services. In particular, several key documents will need to be developed prior to or during the selection process, including the security content to support formal procurement documents such as

- pre-qualification questions and background information for a request for information from potential vendors,
- a statement of requirements, and
- an invitation to tender or request for proposal.

At each stage the customer will need to state, as clearly and accurately as possible, the security requirements that apply to the services in scope. In practice, many organizations have to scramble to prepare or update formal, documented versions of their current security policies, requirements and standards. The most important criteria for such documents is that they are *complete*, *accurate* and *current*, as they will be the initial basis upon which vendors will pitch their bids.

Documents that indicate a lower standard than is currently achieved in practice will lead to misjudged bids, omissions and major inconsistencies when vendors subsequently conduct their own due diligence of the services to be outsourced. Similarly, over-ambitious statements of policies or standards will result in expensive bids. As with many things regarding security in outsourcing, honesty and transparency are the most prudent starting points.

At the end of the selection process, there will no doubt be many points of agreement as well as other points requiring further negotiation with the successful bidder. These will generally be captured in a memorandum of understanding (MOU) before proceeding to the drawing up and negotiation of the formal contract and supporting schedules.

6.3 The importance of due diligence

'Trust, but verify' is a translation of a Russian proverb that was popularized by Ronald Reagan. It concisely summarizes the sensible approach to any proposed outsourcing relationship. Healthy partnerships cannot be built on the basis of constant suspicion, but at the same time it would be dangerous and irresponsible to transfer control of essential services to a complete stranger without first establishing that they are a safe pair of hands.

'Due diligence' is the term commonly used to describe investigations of other companies, especially for the purpose of avoiding a future legal claim. The term entered common usage after the US Securities Act of 1933, which encouraged brokers to exercise due diligence in investigations into companies whose equity they were selling as a defence against legal claims by investors. It is particularly appropriate for outsourcing, as emerging legal and regulatory requirements in the area of data protection are becoming progressively tougher. If a major data breach subsequently occurs, then it will be helpful in any legal defence to be able to demonstrate that an appropriate analysis of risks was carried out, as well as an appropriate set of security checks on the chosen supplier.

A supplier managing a set of outsourced services will have hands-on, day-to-day control of customer assets. Ultimate accountability for their security, however, will continue to remain with the customer. Organizations might prefer to delegate decisions on the level of risk and security to be left to the supplier, but a complete abandonment of responsibility and oversight would be viewed by many outsiders to be an act of negligence, especially if there is critical, valuable or sensitive data at risk.

To safeguard the interests of shareholders, as well as the demands of regulators, it is necessary to conduct a reasonable set of checks to ensure that prospective vendors are both willing and able to deliver the level of security protection that is appropriate to mitigate risks to an acceptable level. Assessing the security capability of suppliers is absolutely essential because the security measures normally applied by service providers can vary considerably, depending on factors such as the supplier's background, the nature of the demands made by previous customers, the security technologies employed, and the skills and experience of managers and staff.

It might seem reasonable to assume that previous customers will have already carried out such checks and hopefully encouraged the supplier to address any major weaknesses identified. Not all customer security requirements are the same, however, and surprisingly few customers actually take the trouble to investigate the security of potential contractors. It is always advisable therefore to carry out your own checks. 'Trust is good, control is better' is a pragmatic piece of advice variously ascribed to Lenin or Stalin. It certainly seems that the Russians have the right kind of questioning mind for assessing potential outsourcers.

6.4 Conducting security checks on suppliers

The challenge in establishing the security credentials of a supplier is in finding the skills, time and resources to conduct an appropriate level of investigation, as well as gaining the cooperation of the supplier. It makes sense to build on existing, publicly available knowledge, but that is unlikely to be sufficient to deliver the level of assurance needed to proceed with a major transfer of assets and services. References from existing customers are a good starting point, but liability considerations might limit the degree of assurance that can be provided.

Many companies giving references take an understandably cautious approach, to ensure that they are scrupulously fair, accurate and not misleading. This is necessary to avoid the possibility of subsequent accusations of negligence or defamation. In fact, it's a fine line to tread. Critical comments might be challenged by the vendor. At the same time, a failure to disclose known problems can also lead to legal action by the customer. Cases in English tort law[6] have acknowledged the need for a duty of care in giving information upon which others rely.

Another clue to the soundness of the vendor is the quality of the customer list, which should to some extent reflect their perceived reliability and capability. If a number of leading banks, government agencies and defence contractors, for example, have bought their services, then there's a good chance that the contractor will have a reasonable understanding of security, as well as the skills, processes and technologies needed to implement it.

---

[6] For example, Hedley Byrne & Co Ltd v Heller & Partners Ltd [1964] AC 465.

Of course, that does not guarantee that these resources will be available to your contract. Nor does it guarantee that the outsourcer will understand the specific security risks, requirements and practices associated with your business or industry sector. Selecting a contractor that has delivered services in the same industry sector, however, is a very sensible choice, as they are more likely to employ practices that are consistent with your own. It's also likely to be cheaper and easier for a contractor to deliver services to an existing, established standard developed for customers with similar requirements, rather than to create an entirely new standard of service.

A range of due diligence services, ranging from security vetting to financial checks, can be obtained from many specialist companies. Commercial managers and legal advisers would be expected to arrange for appropriate checks on a potential vendor's accounts, assets and potential liabilities. Security checks are less common outside the government sector, but many security companies will be willing to conduct a more in-depth review of the security of an overseas service provider, for example. Such services will not come cheap, but might be seen as a prudent measure for a large outsourcing or offshoring contract.

The staff assigned to manage the security of the outsourced services should have an adequate level of security skills and experience. There is a growing shortage of experienced security practitioners, however, so the curriculum vitae of the staff assigned to your contract should be carefully scrutinized to ensure that they have appropriate training, experience and qualifications.

It is important, also, to ensure that you do not immediately lose access to key employees with essential security knowledge and experience that transition to the contractor. Outsourcers will understandably wish to develop promising staff for broader roles in their organization. This process should not be resisted, but the transition should be managed to avoid an impact on services.

Top skills do not come cheap. In any procurement involving the subsequent purchase of contractors at negotiated time and material costs, there is a tendency to aim for the lowest possible day rates. This can be a false economy, as experienced security contractors are more productive, especially when the subject area is complex. It is better to aim for the most efficient service, rather than the lowest price. Measuring value rather than cost is the key. But this is easier said than done, as there are few reliable metrics, and many finance functions will be reluctant to endorse high commercial rates.

6.5 Independent audits and certificates

Previous audits, reviews, accredited certifications or even security marks can also provide a level of confidence, although an endorsement from an unfamiliar previous client, a certificate awarded by an unknown, offshore auditor, or a security mark granted by an obscure third party should never be taken at face value. The standards used and the level of skills and scrutiny applied might not match up to your own expectations, or even to commercially acceptable standards. Some endorsements, of course, are more useful than others.

Accredited certification carried out by an established audit organization against an International Standard is clearly more likely to be reliable than an ad hoc review by an unknown local security vendor. A distinction also needs to be made between the *audit* standard applied and the *security* standard against which the vendor is assessed. Ideally, both need to be based on recognized professional standards.

Certification to BS ISO/IEC 27001, *Information technology – Security techniques – Information security management systems – Requirements* is the most reliable security certification scheme, as it is based on a detailed security specification and involves a professional audit process carried out by an accredited audit body. The process also demands frequent reviews to maintain the certificate. Each certificate will need to be carefully scrutinized, however, to ensure that the target of evaluation and the scope of the certification are appropriate and sufficiently broad to provide confidence in the proposed services offered by the vendor. A certificate awarded to one part of the vendor's organization provides no guarantees that the services offered by other business units will be up to the same standard.

Another popular certification scheme is the SAS 70, an acronym for Statement on Auditing Standard 70. Often mistaken for a security standard, SAS 70 is a widely recognized auditing standard, which is used extensively by outsourcing vendors. This standard was developed several decades ago by the American Institute of Certified Public Accountants. SAS 70 audits are not based on a specification for security controls, but are reports on the 'processing of transactions by service organizations'. Audits are conducted by external auditors, but based on professional standards set by the service provider.

There are, in fact, two types of SAS 70 report. A Type I report examines the controls implemented and gives an opinion on how well the vendor fairly represents its services from a controls perspective. A Type II report is more thorough, and includes an additional section on how effectively the controls operated during a defined period. Questions to ask about an SAS 70 claim are: Which type is it? When was it done? Who did it? What did it cover? SAS 70 provides a degree of confidence, but it is not based on an independent security specification and is not subject to frequent review.

Security marks based on remote testing are also becoming popular to provide confidence in cloud computing services. For example, Veracode, a vendor specializing in security testing technology for applications software, has introduced a security mark to enable Software-as-a-Service suppliers to indicate that their software has been independently security tested using this technology. Such a scheme provides an indication that the service provider applies security standards in software development, but it contains no guarantees about the presence or quality of other security controls.

In fact there is really no substitute for commissioning a professional, independent security review. This can be an expensive option, however, and it would not be feasible to carry out for a long list of potential vendors, or for the purchase of a cloud-based commodity service. It is more appropriate for a major transfer of work to a shortlisted vendor.

Organizations such as small and medium enterprises, that lack the capability and budget to carry out such reviews, should at the very least ask a range of carefully chosen questions to test the supplier's knowledge and understanding of security. Advice from an experienced information security consultancy is invaluable in drawing up sensible questions and evaluating the responses. Examples of the type of basic questions that should be asked of any supplier are listed in the following section.

6.6 Questions to ask a supplier

Each outsourcing contract is different and justifies a bespoke set of questions to draw out the strengths and weaknesses of the potential supplier's security posture and capabilities, especially concerning the range of services, technologies and locations involved in the transfer of work. However, the following questions are essential enquiries that are appropriate to all outsourcing and offshoring contracts.

Selecting a supplier

Questions to ask	Answers to look for
What corporate security policies and standards have you adopted and implemented? How extensively have these policies and standards been implemented?	Look for the use of internationally recognized standards such as BS ISO/IEC 27001, and a portfolio of policies that is regularly updated. Ensure that corporate policies and standards will also apply to the services delivered to you.
How do you go about checking that your security policies and standards are actually being applied? How often is this done?	Look for the use of formal, independent audits by qualified auditors. Audits should be conducted at least annually.
Who is responsible for security generally within your organization, and specifically for this contract? What experience do they possess? To whom do they report?	Ensure there is a responsible, qualified and experienced senior manager in charge of security generally and especially for the services to be delivered. The reporting point should be to at least a member of the management team responsible for the contract to ensure that security issues can be quickly escalated.
How are security risks to customer services assessed? How frequently is this done? Who is responsible for this process?	Look for a formal system that enables local risk assessments to be carried out under the oversight of a corporate risk assessment process, reporting to a senior management board.
What level of qualifications, training and experience do security practitioners possess? Is there a minimum standard or a professional development programme?	Look for the existence of a professional development scheme underpinned by internationally recognized professional qualifications. Minimum standards should be applied for the recruitment and deployment of individual security staff.
What types of security technologies have been implemented?	A good outsourcer should deploy a broad range of security technologies including secure remote access, encryption, content filtering and scanning, intrusion detection, activity monitoring, and identity and access management.

Questions to ask	Answers to look for
How do you go about vulnerability management? How often are platforms scanned for security vulnerabilities? How long does it take to apply a new operating system patch? How frequently are anti-malware signatures updated?	Prompt implementation of critical patches and anti-malware signature updates are both essential, as are daily scans of Internet-facing platforms and regular scans of internal platforms. The time taken to implement new patches provides an indication of the ability of the outsourcer to react to new threats and vulnerabilities.
Is there a business continuity management process and plans?	Outsourcers need to respond to customer requirements for business continuity plans but they also need to have a planning process of their own to cover disasters, failures or major security breaches.
How are major incidents managed? Is there a crisis team? Is it regularly exercised? Who is in charge of this process?	All services providers require a formal process to manage events, incidents and crises of all sizes and scopes. This demands a formal hierarchy of crisis teams and reporting points, which must be regularly rehearsed, and report into a senior executive board representative.
How are company staff made aware of security risk, corporate policies and compliance requirements?	Look for security induction and ongoing security awareness and briefing programmes. Ideally, staff should sign off their understanding and acceptance of an 'acceptable use' policy.

6.7 Security selection criteria

To select the most suitable bidder requires more than just an assurance that they are competent to deliver the assigned services in a secure fashion. It also requires an appropriate set of criteria for rating the capability of each bidder. This set of criteria will inevitably be similar to the questions listed above, as they both reflect critical security issues for an award of contract. They will, however, be judged from a different perspective, i.e. one concerned primarily with comparison, rather than fact-finding.

Selecting a supplier

The following list is provided as an example of the areas that are known to provide a good indication of the security capabilities of suppliers. Each contract, however, is unique and will demand adjustments in the relative importance and weighting assigned to each criterion.

- Senior management commitment to information security: how senior, how significant and how effectively communicated and implemented.
- Quality and coverage of policies and standards: how similar, comprehensive and realistic, and how well implemented.
- Skills and experience of security staff: the level of standards sought and implemented.
- Capability to identify, assess and mitigate security risks: the degree of knowledge, skills and experience, and the speed of response to new risks.
- Understanding and identification of relevant legal and regulatory compliance requirements: how well the outsourcer understands relevant legal and compliance requirements, and how capable they appear to be in implementing them.
- Quality of information security management system: how it benchmarks against International Standards such as BS ISO/IEC 27001, and how well it appears to be working.
- Physical security of premises: how effective this appears to be within the context of the broader range of customer requirements.
- Personnel checks and controls: the standards demanded and the checks applied to all staff that will be deployed on the contract.
- Quality of audit, inspection and certification processes: the quality of the internal audit or external certification processes, as well as the perceived management response to identified problems.
- Availability and use of security technologies: the availability of licences, skills and experience for implementing specialist security technologies.
- Vulnerability management capability: the speed, frequency and coverage of vulnerability scanning, patch management and anti-malware updates for platforms delivering customer services, and whether the need for penetration testing has been addressed.
- Incident response capability: the structure, experience and maturity of the incident and crisis management teams, as well as the perceived effectiveness of the interface with customer organizations.

It is also important to plan for the fact that the results of the security assessment will need to be incorporated into the overall decision-making process for supplier selection. Security can be treated as a mandatory criterion, where a minimum level is required, or it can be a contributory factor to a broader decision taking account of cost, functionality and technical excellence. It is clearly better that the supplier selection takes place with full awareness of the implications of a failure to meet security standards, rather than dealing with a consequential situation where a security manager is forced to raise a 'red flag' and lobby senior management for a reversal of a selection board recommendation.

6.8 Learning points from this chapter

This chapter has explored the security considerations associated with selecting an outsourcing supplier. Key learning points to note can be summarized as follows.

▶ The starting point for security managers is to consider how security considerations are best incorporated into the supplier selection process, and what information is needed to enable potential suppliers to prepare bids. The selection process generally begins with a request for information or proposals setting out objectives, requirements and expectations.

▶ Invitations to suppliers should include an overview of security policies and standards, and indicate the information to be provided and the selection criteria. Security input is needed to support pre-qualification questions, statements of requirements and other information to support the invitation to suppliers.

▶ Further documentation can be provided through a team room. This is usually online and must be securely designed to safeguard the information and prevent users from becoming aware of the identities of other bidders. Documents will need to be complete, accurate and current, as they will form the initial basis for vendor bids.

▶ Security checks will be needed on the reliability and capability of shortlisted bidders. This reduces risks, safeguards the interests of shareholders, and helps meet the demands of regulators. Assessing the capability of suppliers is essential because security measures applied by vendors varies widely, according to the supplier's background, the nature of previous customer demands, and the skills and security technologies employed.

▶ Due diligence starts with publicly available knowledge, references from existing customers, and inspection of the quality of the vendor's customer list. Contractors that have delivered services in the same industry sector are likely to have a good understanding of sector requirements. Previous audits, reviews and certifications provide a degree of confidence, though their provenance should be carefully checked.

▶ Accredited certification, carried out by an established audit organization against an International Standard, is more reliable than an ad hoc review by an unknown local security vendor. SAS 70 is a popular audit standard, but is based on standards set by the supplier. In fact, there is no substitute for commissioning a professional, independent security review, but this is an expensive option, and not feasible for a lengthy list of vendors or for a cloud-based commodity service.

▶ Small and medium enterprises without the capability and budget to conduct such reviews should ask a range of carefully chosen questions to test the supplier's knowledge and understanding of security. Advice from an experienced consultancy will help. Examples of suitable questions and suggested selection criteria are given in this chapter. Areas to address include the levels/capability of management commitment, policies and standards, skills and experience, risk management, management systems, physical and personnel security, auditing, use of security technologies, vulnerability management and incident response capability.

7 Developing and negotiating the contract

7.1 The importance of a good contract

The contract is the primary opportunity for the customer organization to specify what it demands and expects over the lifetime of the partnership. Once signed, further changes will be subject to negotiation. It is likely to be relatively expensive to introduce subsequent additions or variations.

The contract will also set the tone for the longer-term relationship. A prescriptive specification, for example, will encourage a more formal, distant and perhaps less flexible response to service delivery. On the other hand, a more general statement of requirements is likely to encourage an interactive partnership, with potentially greater innovation and flexibility, but also more argument about how to translate business problems and expressed requirements into delivered services.

It is important, therefore, to pay close attention to detail when negotiating the contract. It warrants a special effort by both sides and it justifies seeking the best possible advice and assigning the best available resources.

When customers first enter negotiations with an outsourcer, there is often a tendency to assume that they will be up against a top team of expert lawyers. After all, the outsourcing company or consortium will be more experienced in negotiating outsourcing contracts. The expectation of many business managers is that the supplier will run rings around the customer in negotiations. In fact, it is quite possible to gain the edge over the supplier in contract negotiations. Strategy and good advice is all that it takes.

The first recommendation is to hire the best outside expertise that can be obtained. A team of external specialists focusing on a single objective will generally be more than a match for a team of busy, in-house lawyers. The second is not to be rushed into an agreement and to hold out for what you need, for as long as possible, as the vendor will generally be keener than you to close the deal quickly and therefore more inclined to compromise.

When considering the process of contract development, three key questions to ask are:

Developing and negotiating the contract

1) What approach should be taken to framing and agreeing the contract, who should be involved, and how can security specialists contribute?
2) What other documents will be needed, other than the main contract, and what resources and experience will be required?
3) How should the security requirements be specified, communicated and incorporated?

A good starting point is to commence with a clear understanding of the characteristics of a good contract. A good contract has two key attributes. Firstly, it is one that clearly specifies the services required, how they will be delivered, and who will be responsible for delivering them. Secondly, it should also define the processes to manage changes, rectify non-compliant deliverables, and resolve potential disputes. These are the fundamental building blocks of any successful commercial partnership. Yet, surprisingly, many organizations fail to address these points adequately.

Contracts also need to be comprehensive and unambiguous, in order to avoid uncertainty and potential misinterpretation. At the same time, they must be adaptable to cater for future changes. This requirement is especially important for information security, where new requirements, such as new threats and compliance demands, and new solutions, such as new technologies and recommended management processes, are continually emerging.

Who should draw up the contract? Traditionally, most contracts for general purchases of IT products and services will have been drawn up and negotiated by commercial managers and legal advisers, based on functional requirements set by business or IT managers. Outsourcing contracts, however, present much higher risks and often involve longer, deeper and more complex partnerships. That demands greater input from and engagement with security professionals, either in-house security managers or external consultants. It also requires a set of specialist contract schedules to define the security policies, standards and controls that must be applied. These schedules are specialist documents and should therefore be drafted and negotiated by subject matter experts, with appropriate advice from commercial and legal specialists.

Outsourcing contract negotiations need to go much further and deeper than just agreeing a specification for the services to be delivered. They must also aim to agree a set of defined policies, standards and processes that are reasonable and acceptable to all parties. A degree of alignment will be required by both sides. No matter how much purchasing power and leverage a customer might have over a supplier, it is simply not realistic to expect another organization to adopt new working practices without a major upheaval. New processes also take time to mature: at least several months, and in some cases several years.

That also implies that if the outsourcer's existing security management practices or risk tolerance levels fall well short of your own standards, then it's unlikely that the partnership will succeed. No organization can become proficient in security overnight, no matter how hard they try or how much money they're prepared to spend.

7.2 Steps in negotiating the contract

The negotiation stage requires a strong input from both end-user business managers and functional experts if it is to establish the foundations for a successful partnership. Negotiating the contract should not be left in the hands of in-house commercial and legal specialists, though their extensive knowledge and experience is absolutely essential to the process.

In practice I have found that the most successful approach in preparing an outsourcing contract is to first get the appropriate business stakeholders and subject matter experts to define their requirements in clear, plain English, and then to allow the lawyers to apply the necessary legal and commercial enhancements.

This simple rationale behind this method is that lawyers cannot be expected to identify and define business and technical requirements; equally, subject matter experts will lack the skill to express their requirements in a legally binding way. The same approach should also be applied to face-to-face negotiations: get the subject matter experts to explain and agree their requirements, then leave it to the lawyers to apply the necessary legal touches. It is certainly worth investing the time to train legal advisers in the terminology and finer points of information security in order to gain their maximum support.

In fact, the contract negotiation process is much less intimidating than many security professionals generally expect. A good contract is not built on hard, commercial bargaining, but on practical, common-sense agreements between practitioners, supported by commercial and legal advice that translates the business aspirations into binding contractual commitments. Getting this right involves three main things: a proactive strategy, an appreciation of negotiating tactics and a logical development process.

Developing and negotiating the contract

In practice, unfortunately, few customers take the trouble to develop a clear strategy and most tend to cut short or omit many vital steps because of time pressure, budgetary constraints, or political expediency. Time and effort invested at this stage in an outsourcing programme, however, is a smart and prudent investment. Typical steps in an ideal process might include the following.

- Develop a strategy that takes account of the business motives and objectives for the outsourcing.
- Propose and agree a process and timetable with the outsourcer.
- Make arrangements for an appropriate level of specialist, external legal or commercial support, as required.
- Identify and gain the cooperation of a set of in-house or external subject matter experts, and brief them on their role, as well as the key principles of successful contract negotiation.
- Assign lawyers to draft the main contract, with subject matter experts drafting the supporting schedules.
- Check, improve and agree all documents before sending to the outsourcer for comments.
- Sit down with the outsourcer and decide the agreed text, with subject matter experts taking the lead and lawyers supporting the process.
- Finalize and approve the contract and schedules.

In many organizations this will appear to be a radical departure from conventional contract development processes. But that is the nature of outsourcing and offshoring: it is a radical initiative that warrants a radical approach to its management.

It is important to remember that contract negotiation, especially when it comes to security, should not be a combative process. Both sides need, and should want, the contract to work. It's essential to look after the organization's interests and aim to strike the best deal, but this should not be at the expense of the interests of the overall partnership.

A further consideration is the role that is often played by external consultants. In-house staff have day jobs and will struggle to find the time to support contract development. They might have extensive knowledge of IT systems and business processes, but lack the skills and the time to develop formal contract documentation. External consultants are not a direct substitute for in-house staff, but offer a complementary capability. They should work closely with in-house experts to translate their knowledge into contract specifications, and to identify and fill gaps in corporate memory and experience, for example where knowledge of legacy systems and processes is weak or has been lost.

7.3 Negotiating strategy and tactics

Negotiation is an art that has been studied and practised for thousands of years by diplomats, salesmen and customers. Yet, surprisingly, the state-of-the-art remains relatively simple and many business executives are unskilled in its finer points. Negotiators can employ a range of different strategies and tactics, but careful preparation and planning, together with good diplomacy and patience are the real secrets to achieving the most successful possible outcome.

In fact, the negotiation process involves several distinct stages, beginning (as always) with a period of preparation, then proceeding through information exchange and bargaining until a commitment by both parties is finally achieved. Advance planning and preparation is needed to identify the best appropriate strategy, and to prepare the necessary supporting documentation. Information exchange will generally start with a draft contract and a set of draft supporting schedules, which will need to be prepared by the customer.

The opening proposal needs to be factually correct as far as the specification of services is concerned. But in other respects, it might be pitched ambitiously: perhaps aimed high to prepare the ground for a subsequent compromise. Alternatively, it might be submitted as a fair, reasonable, take-it-or-leave-it proposal, not intended to be open to further bargaining.

Whether an organization chooses to adopt the former strategy or the latter position will depend on many factors, such as corporate culture, degree of empowerment, bargaining room, personality and constraints on time, money and resources. Because of the need to encourage suppliers to 'go the extra mile', security is best negotiated in an open, honest manner; but specific points often need to be negotiated in a harder, more competitive fashion in order to ensure that the best possible outcome is achieved.

Negotiation preferences differ across countries and cultures, with a marked difference between the methodical approach that is generally practised in the West, and the more creative style that is often encountered in the East. Japanese executives, for example, are excellent at considering the total package and creatively trading-off particular elements or groups of options in order to build a win/win outcome. In contrast, American executives are more inclined to work through each page of the draft contract in turn, aiming to gain the maximum advantage for each clause.

Most people tend to adopt a negotiating style based on their individual preferences. Professor G. Richard Shell of Wharton Business School at the University of Pennsylvania has identified five distinct negotiating styles: the *avoider* (of conflict); the *compromiser*; the *accommodator*; the *competitor*; and the *problem solver*. In practice, people will apply a mixture of these styles depending on their personality and experience. People who share the same negotiation style will tend to understand each other better, which generally leads to a more positive outcome. For this reason, a change of personnel can often improve negotiations that have begun to stall. Personality, attitude and skills are major influencing factors in any negotiation.

There are several negotiating techniques that can be exploited, some of which are generally applied instinctively and others consciously adopted. Many tactics include the exploitation of emotions, for example through displays of anger, veiled threats or sympathy. Another classic technique is the use of a 'good cop/bad cop' tactic, where a sympathetic negotiator follows on from an aggressive one to help solicit concessions.

Negotiating tactics may also involve subtle techniques such as deliberately conceding a number of minor issues in the hope of building leverage for a more important concession. It is also possible, though not recommended, to gain a degree of success from being as uncompromising as possible in the hope of gaining concessions by simply wearing down the other party. Patience, combined with quiet determination, is likely to prove a more effective tactic for a customer negotiating with a supplier who is keen to close a deal to help achieve a bonus target.

The most successful negotiations, however, are the ones that are open, honest and creative, and which strive to find or create a set of advantages for both parties. Achieving this might involve a degree of advance consensus on negotiating principles and rules of engagement.

The feasibility of such an approach succeeding, however, will depend primarily on the attitudes and behaviour of the negotiators. But setting preconditions for discussions can help to shape the overall perception, attitude and behaviour associated with the discussions, and to manage expectations. Another useful option is to use an independent third party, who might be able to explore a greater range of possible scenarios without creating a hostage to fortune by proposing possible, acceptable compromises.

Many contract negotiations become progressively adversarial. This phenomenon is one that should be avoided as far as possible. A win/lose outcome, or so-called 'zero-sum game', is bad for both the future relationship and the quality of services delivered. If the customer drives too hard a bargain, the services will be adversely impacted. On the other hand, if the vendor extracts too high a price, the services will not represent best value for money. In particular, security will suffer in any adversarial relationship, as conflict and tension will discourage informal cooperation, which is essential for encouraging informal reporting of risks or incidents, and for persuading the vendor's staff to implement preventative or corrective actions that might fall outside the scope of the contract.

In fact, security is a difficult requirement to negotiate for several reasons. Firstly, if assessed correctly, there is generally little room for compromise. If a security measure is deemed essential, then it will need to be applied; whereas if it is merely desirable, then it is unlikely to be justified.

Secondly, it is rare to encounter organizations who share identical security practices and perception of security risks. There will inevitably be significant differences in the views of both sides on the level of security and the nature of countermeasures required. These variations will need to be considered carefully and sympathetically.

Thirdly, not all security measures can be quickly, easily or economically implemented. There are always technical, financial or operational constraints that will prevent particular controls from being applied in practice. Patience with firmness and persistence will be required to push through many important security improvements. Managers negotiating security conditions will need to be fully alert to such issues.

On the positive side, however, security is a requirement that can often be satisfied in several different ways. There are numerous opportunities for alternative control solutions. A little creative thinking can often identify perfectly acceptable compensating controls that can be applied more easily, if a particular control specified by the customer cannot be met by the vendor.

Physical and procedural security measures can, for example, provide a cruder but potentially acceptable alternative solution to an encryption requirement. Similarly, the implementation of enhanced monitoring controls can often help to mitigate the risks presented by an undesirable but unavoidable level access to sensitive data by the contractor. The use of new, emerging technologies can also be explored, which in some cases might offer a solution that is better for both parties.

Security is a subject that generally responds well to creative negotiations that aim to satisfy the interests of both sides. Such an approach is a smarter and more effective strategy than simply aiming to beat the other party into submission. Achieving a win/win result is also easier than many managers might imagine, especially when negotiating large contracts, as there will be many requirements that are important to one party but not to the other, providing opportunities for efficient trades. Each party will also possess a range of facilities, skills and intellectual property, which might usefully be extended to the partner, at relatively low cost. If such opportunities can be identified and successfully traded, then the expectations of both parties will be exceeded.

Developing an effective long-term security relationship requires a degree of freedom from the constraints of the contract, in order to address risks and issues that were unforeseen at the contract negotiation stage. Such future flexibility needs to be borne in mind when negotiating the contract.

A tough, uncompromising approach might set the wrong tone for the long-term partnership. Trust and confidence are the foundations of a successful relationship. At the same time, it is important to be realistic, and recognize that verbal promises and future aspirations might not be guaranteed, and that the climate of the relationship can quickly change from warmly cooperative to cool or adversarial, especially following the signing of a contract, or when there is a change of staff on either side of the partnership.

7.4 Ensuring confidentiality and privacy of data

Ensuring the confidentiality and privacy of sensitive data across an outsourced supply chain is an immensely difficult task that should never be underestimated. Security policies, standards and contracts alone cannot ensure it. In day-to-day practice, short-term operational and financial demands will often override the best intentions of managers struggling to adhere to unfamiliar new security rules. Policies therefore need to be reinforced by continuous education, vigilance and audit. The following mechanisms can also help.

- A security classification system (see Chapter 4) will help to differentiate sensitive data that requires more secure handling.
- Maintaining a map of where sensitive data is stored and processed helps to pinpoint where additional checks and controls are needed.
- Data leakage prevention technology can help to identify and control flows of sensitive data across network perimeters.

In particular, especially when considering an offshoring initiative, it should be noted that national laws on data protection and privacy legislation are not exactly consistent across the globe. Some, in fact, are contradictory. The contract must ensure that the supplier is required to comply with relevant local law, in a manner enforceable against them.

The demands of many individual laws will at some point, of course, need to be considered and satisfied. From an overall governance perspective, however, it is generally easier and more efficient to aim, as far as possible, to implement a single, high overall standard of data protection and privacy safeguards across all regions, rather than attempt to manage varying levels of control in order to satisfy the minimum requirements of local jurisdictions. Managing a patchwork quilt of compliance is a complex and potentially fruitless overhead in a global compliance environment that is becoming progressively tougher, and converging around common minimum standards of best practice.

The termination or planned exit from an outsourcing arrangement will also need to be considered at the contract stage, and negotiated accordingly. In particular, it's important to gain guarantees for the safe return or assured destruction of all sensitive data and valuable intellectual property, including security assets such as authentication devices, as well as essential management items such as instruction manuals and encryption key material. Chapter 11 addresses the specific security risks, requirements and issues associated with the eventual, inevitable termination of the contract.

7.5 Building flexibility for future change

The contract will need to accommodate many future changes in response to new security requirements, whether demanded by customers, regulators or other stakeholders, or in response to new threats and vulnerabilities. Post-contract changes inevitably attract high charges, so it's important to agree defined processes for the periodic review and refreshment of security policies, standards and controls. Security will also need to be maintained throughout future restructures, relocations or subcontracting of services, included those initiated by the contractor. The contract should therefore ensure that legal and regulatory requirements are binding across both current and future organizations, sites and subcontracts.

A further consideration is the level of detail in specifications, which is useful to articulate requirements but which can also potentially act as a constraint to business and security agility. Contracts need to be comprehensive and unambiguous, but an overly prescriptive approach might set the wrong tone, discouraging future initiatives by the contractor and thereby inhibiting potential flexibility.

A prescriptive approach, however, might be both necessary and appropriate for short-term offshore contracts, where the outsourcer is expected to deliver no more than the service that is specified. Each contract needs, therefore, to be considered on its own merits, but there are some techniques that can encourage an optimal balance of flexibility and assurance.

Linking contractual requirements to recognized International Standards, for example, reduces the risk of countermeasures becoming obsolete, as standards are periodically refreshed and updated. A further enabler of flexibility is the use of risk assessment methods that deliver an output indicating a level of security that needs to be met without specifying how it should be delivered, rather than a prescriptive set of controls. Implemented and managed correctly, such an approach offers the capability to select new security controls to meet new or evolving risks.

This approach, however, demands a high degree of trust and involvement on both sides in order to avoid the possibility of the supplier exploiting this flexibility to minimize the security measures needed to respond to identified security risks. It is important, therefore, to ensure that the method used for assessing and responding to risks is appropriate, and agreed in advance. It is also important to ensure that the ownership rights for any new methodologies developed by the supplier for the purposes of the contract are also shared by the customer. This is needed to help build a consistent approach to security governance across the customer organization, enabling the same methods to be applied by other third-party contractors, as well as for other purposes including risk assessments and other reviews and governance processes that are performed outside of the scope of the contract.

The primary objective should be to ensure that ultimate accountability for assessment and management of risk and security lies with the customer. If services are outsourced to multiple contractors it is not prudent or feasible to leave security management (or the techniques applied) in the hands of a single supplier, unless there is a clear intention to subcontract a range of enterprise security services to a particular, chosen suppler.

7.6 Developing the security schedule

7.6.1 General points

Corporate policies and standards are generally set on the basis of considerations such as customer expectations, compliance requirements and the business impact of incidents. The supplier will, however, be subject to a different set of requirements and might therefore have a different perspective on what constitutes an acceptable level of risks and controls. The vendor must therefore be persuaded to implement and provide services in accordance with the customer's security policies and standards rather than their own.

The security schedule will need to define the scope of the security measures that the vendor must implement in order to maintain an acceptable, overall level of security protection for the organization's information and services. It should also define the specific security policies, standards and practices that are needed to ensure consistency with the organization's governance processes and security architecture. There are, in fact, several sets of security requirements.

First, there are a range of general control requirements needed to meet corporate policies and standards, for example those based on the application of BS ISO/IEC 27000, with appropriate interpretation for a particular environment, technology, level of risk or local circumstances. Responsibility for those controls will need to be divided appropriately between the customer, as user, and the supplier, as IT services provider.

Second, there will also be a number of specific security requirements, implemented to safeguard a particular set of information assets against a specific set of risks. These measures might not be adequately addressed by existing policies and standards, and should therefore be listed in the security schedule. The contract should require that all security requirements existing at the start date of the contract are maintained to safeguard customer systems and assets for which the vendor will have responsibility, except where an alternative set of measures has been agreed. In particular, the contract should insist that any security certificates existing as at the commencement of the contract should be maintained, as these require a major investment to achieve and, if left to lapse, might be expensive to regain.

Third, the contract should also require that security policies and standards are applied to all new developments, as well as to changes to systems and environments, unless otherwise agreed. The contract will also need to ensure that the security requirement specified in the contract schedules extend to all subcontractors and third parties introduced by the contractor, including the need to sign an agreed non-disclosure agreement and to return or destroy all information when it is no longer required.

All outsourcing initiatives should aim to maintain and continually improve the level of quality of services delivered. Quality management processes and initiatives are also enablers of good security management. The contract should require that the contractor operates (and requires its subcontractors to operate) a quality management system consistent with good industry practice.

During the subsequent transition stage, it will be necessary for both parties to jointly review all outstanding audit actions and agree the priorities and methods for progressing each of these issues. Ideally the necessary action should be progressed through an agreed remedial plan, which will need to be supported by an agreed level of budget and resources. Both parties will need to agree the priorities for such improvements, as well as the methodologies used for carrying out the improvements. Advance agreement on the level of resource assigned to this work is a useful device to incorporate into the contract to prevent the contractor from exploiting the need for change with an excessive charge.

The general security requirements in the contract schedule should be based, as far as possible, on established public standards such as the BS ISO/IEC 27000 standards. Public standards are better understood and supported by external service providers. These security standards will need to be carefully applied, with appropriate professional interpretation by both the customer and contractor, taking account of environmental and technological levels of risk as well as local circumstances and practices.

Examples of the range of control requirements that would be appropriate to include in a security schedule are listed below. These requirements are primarily based on BS ISO/IEC 27002, *Information technology – Security techniques –*

Code of practice for information security management and follow its contents structure. Use of a well-recognized checklist such as this will save time and effort for the outsourcer, who will generally be familiar with this structure. It will also reduce the possibility of the outsourcer overlooking any individual requirements that might, for example, be listed under an unfamiliar heading.

An important point to note is that BS ISO/IEC 27002 is written in a neutral style, in that it does not apportion responsibility for meeting its requirements. Each individual requirement will therefore need to be interpreted to define which party will be held accountable for meeting it. Not all requirements will fall to the contractor. Many responsibilities will need to be assigned to the customer organization and taken account of when designing the future organization and governance processes.

7.6.2 Security policy

The contractor should be required to communicate the customer's security policy and standards to all relevant personnel as well as to any subcontractors involved in the delivery of the services. The latter point concerning subcontractors is important for the contractor to note, as it will involve additional costs that might not otherwise have been accounted for in the contractor's bid.

7.6.3 Organization of information security

The contractor should be required to assign specific organizational accountabilities, roles and responsibilities for all aspects of security to appropriate managers, committees and staff, including for example

- a senior management forum to review and approve policy, responsibilities, risks and incidents, as well as approving any initiatives to enhance information security,
- the allocation of specific responsibilities for the security of individual IT projects, information assets and information security management processes,
- the allocation of responsibility for authorization and control of access, including third parties and subcontractors, to the organization's information systems, infrastructure and buildings,
- the allocation of responsibilities for reviewing and managing the security of activities and assets outsourced, subcontracted or assigned to the outsourcer.

- authorization processes for the secure introduction of new information systems and infrastructure,
- access to sources of specialist, authoritative information security advice,
- the allocation of responsibilities, contacts and processes for reporting and managing security incidents, and
- the allocation of responsibility for reviewing organizational practice against policy and standards.

The outsourcer should be required to ensure that all employees or subcontractors engaged in security activities have appropriate professional security training, experience and qualifications. Minimum standards or benchmarks should be agreed by both parties, as well as responsibilities for bearing the costs of any additional training that is required. This can be a contentious point, especially if the contractor is aiming to cut costs, or planning to introduce junior staff to the customer contract for professional development purposes.

7.6.4 Asset management

The contractor should be required to implement and maintain appropriate inventories of the assets utilized in delivering services under their control. Sensitive and critical information will need to be classified by the customer and protected by the contractor in accordance with specified information classification guidelines. The contractor should also be required to notify the customer of any proposed changes to infrastructure or systems that may have an impact on the confidentiality, integrity or availability of the customer's information or services.

7.6.5 Human resources security

The contractor should be required to implement and maintain appropriate controls to reduce the risks of human error, theft, fraud or misuse of facilities in accordance with corporate security policies or standards. Ideally, these should include

- personnel screening at the recruitment stage,
- security and confidentiality obligations in subcontracts, as well as terms and conditions of staff employment,
- staff security education and training (including cooperating with customer security awareness campaigns),

- security incident reporting and response,
- maintaining a disciplinary process for employees who have violated security policies and procedures, and
- monitoring system usage and maintaining audit logs to detect and report on breaches of security policy or misuse of systems.

The level of personnel screening that is appropriate will depend on the nature of the work being outsourced. If the work is of a classified government nature, attracting a security classification such as 'Confidential' or 'Secret', then there will be a legal requirement to protect it under the Official Secrets Act and to ensure that personnel are vetted to the required government standard. For commercial security purposes, it is more appropriate to use a public code of practice such as BS 7858, *Security screening of individuals employed in a security environment – Code of practice*[7] for personnel employed in activities that either require access to sensitive client data or involve significant control over critical client business services.

The contractor should also be required to cooperate with customer security investigations and internal disciplinary processes. Ideally this should be done at no extra cost. A formal process and code of practice for conducting such investigations will need to be agreed by both parties. The contractor should be required not to withhold any information needed to support a formal security or disciplinary investigation. The contractor will also require an assurance from the customer that such information provided will not be used for other purposes. Liabilities should also be addressed regarding any claims arising as a result of the investigation.

7.6.6 Physical and environmental security

The contractor should be required to implement and maintain appropriate physical and environmental security controls, in order to prevent unauthorized access, damage and interference to business premises and information at the

---

[7] Among other things, BS 7858 advises that potential employees should be required to sign an appropriate application form declaration, and to provide proof of identity and address, details of education, employment and criminal convictions, and character references.

---

premises utilized in the provision of services, in accordance with corporate security policies and standards. Ideally these should include

- physical security perimeters and entry controls,
- arrangements for securing specific sensitive areas, such as offices, rooms and facilities,
- appropriate sites and protection of equipment to reduce environmental threats, hazards and opportunities for unauthorized access,
- protection of power supplies and data cables,
- equipment maintenance considerations,
- secure disposal or purging of equipment before re-use,
- clear desk and clear screen policy, and
- controls to prevent unauthorized removal of equipment.

The contract should require that the contractor's staff comply with the organization's security policies and standards whilst on corporate premises. It should also insist on an appropriate level or physical or logical separation of information, data and systems from that of its other customers, in order to prevent the possibility of any unauthorized access to them.

7.6.7 Communications and operations management

The contractor should be required to maintain appropriate controls, procedures and operating instructions to ensure the correct and secure operation of information processing facilities in accordance with relevant corporate security policies and standards. These should include

- maintaining the documented operating procedures for the execution of each job, including housekeeping activities,
- operational change control processes,
- incident management procedures,
- segregation of duties where appropriate,
- separation of development and operational facilities,
- control of external facilities management,
- system planning and acceptance processes,
- controls to protect against malicious software, including computer viruses,
- controlled housekeeping processes, including information back-up, maintenance of operator logs and fault logging,
- network management controls,

- secure management, handling and disposal of media, information and documentation, and
- controls over exchanges of information and software with other organizations, including exchange agreements, security of media in transit, and controls to safeguard electronic exchanges.

7.6.8 Access control

The contractor should be required to maintain appropriate controls to control access to information and business processes in accordance with relevant corporate security policies and standards. These controls will need to cover every step from initial user registration through to cancellation of registration when the user no longer needs to access the system or service in question. They should include

- documented access control policies,
- management of user access, including processes and controls to register users, manage passwords, control privileged access and regularly review access rights,
- procedures and education for users, including guidance on the selection, use and security of passwords, and the protection of unattended user equipment,
- network access controls, including appropriate policies and controls to authenticate users/nodes and to segregate and route network traffic,
- operating system access controls, including appropriate measures to authenticate and control users/terminals and to control system utilities,
- application access controls based on defined access policies,
- monitoring system access and use, including event logging and usage monitoring with accurate time stamping, and
- control of mobile computing and teleworking.

7.6.9 Information systems acquisition, development and maintenance

The contractor should be required to maintain appropriate processes and controls to ensure that security is built into information systems, in accordance with relevant corporate security policies and standards. These will include

- a security requirements analysis, based on a risk assessment, to identify all relevant controls,
- input data validation controls,

- internal processing checks and controls,
- message authentication controls where appropriate,
- output data validation checks,
- cryptographic controls, including (where appropriate) encryption, digital signatures, non-repudiation services and key management services,
- control of systems files, including operational software, test data and program source libraries, and
- security in development and support processes, including change control, technical reviews of operating system changes, restrictions on changes to packages and measures to prevent or detect the introduction of covert channels or Trojan code.

The contractor should also be required to ensure that new systems are consistent with the requirements or recommendations of any security architecture or cryptographic security policy maintained by the customer organization.

7.6.10 Information security incident management

The contractor should be required to ensure that appropriate incident management measures are maintained, including

- formal incident management procedures, supported by appropriate training for staff,
- agreed timeframes for reporting, responding to and resolving identified security incidents, and
- appropriate processes and controls to prevent or reduce the impact of and future occurrences of identified security incidents.

The contractor should be required to maintain appropriate intelligence feeds for monitoring and responding to new security alerts, including vulnerability and virus warnings. Security patches should be implemented within agreed time periods depending on the level of criticality. It is also important to learn from past incidents in order to identify and eradicate the underlying causes and thereby help to prevent similar incidents happening in the future. A root cause analysis should therefore be carried out for all major security incidents and all findings, recommendations and actions discussed and agreed with the customer.

The contractor should be required to maintain records of events and incidents of security interest and to compile periodic reports for the customer, summarising the types and numbers of such incidents. Typical useful items to report might include data breaches, misuse of systems, levels of malware, equipment losses and levels of customer helpdesk enquires for password resets. It is also important to ensure that information such as threat intelligence that might impact business operations and continuity planning is shared with the customer.

7.6.11 Business continuity management

The contractor should be required to implement and maintain appropriate controls to protect the critical business processes that support the services to be delivered from the effects of major failures and disasters in accordance with relevant corporate security policies and standards. These should include

- a business continuity management process,
- continuity and impact analyses for major potential hazards,
- business continuity plans, where appropriate, for critical business processes,
- a framework for maintaining business continuity plans, and
- testing, maintenance and re-assessment processes.

In practice, both the customer and service provider are likely to operate enterprise-wide processes for managing business continuity and responding to emergencies, disasters and crises. During the transition periods, each party should be required to examine their respective processes for business continuity and crisis management, identify opportunities for any harmonization of processes, define appropriate interfaces and agree how any issues should be progressed.

7.6.12 Regulatory compliance

The contractor should be required to implement and maintain appropriate controls to avoid potential breaches of any criminal and civil law or contractual obligation, in accordance with relevant corporate security policies and standards. These should include

- identification of all applicable laws, regulations or contractual requirements,
- controls to prevent infringement of intellectual property rights, including software copyright,
- safeguarding of organizational records from loss, destruction and falsification,
- policies to ensure data protection and privacy of personal information,
- prevention of misuse of information processing facilities,

- regulation of cryptographic controls,
- guidance on the collection of evidence to support legal actions, and
- regular reviews of compliance of systems and processes with the organization's corporate security policy.

The contractor should be required to demonstrate, at least annually, that the customer's security requirements are being comprehensively applied across all systems, infrastructure and business processes used in delivering the specified services. This will need to be achieved to an agreed standard, through an agreed process, and ideally carried out by an approved independent body. The contract should also ensure that where compliance failures are identified, there is an agreed process and timetable to implement any necessary remedial measures. The contractor should also be required to maintain any accredited certifications and to cooperate in any plans to extend the scope of these certifications.

The customer should retain the right to audit any procedures, policies or standards established by the contractor or its subcontractors to ensure that the required standards have been met. The contractor should also agree to cooperate with any security reviews, tests or audits carried out by the customer or its agents. This is best done through the development of an agreed code of practice for audits and reviews to ensure that both parties work together to minimize the potential for excessive intrusions or non-cooperation.

The contract should also ensure that the customer organization is entitled to commission or carry out regular 'penetration' security tests to determine the security profile of its infrastructure, in order to identify potential weaknesses that might be exploited. This is a difficult area as contractors are generally reluctant to encourage intrusive tests by outside parties, some of whom might be regarded as potential competitors. It is helpful to agree in advance a list of suitable contractors to carry out this work, to ensure that cooperation is not withheld. Responsibility for the consequences of the tests, including remedial action as well as any adverse impact on service levels, will also need to be clarified and agreed by both parties.

7.7 Customer responsibilities

A good contract is not just a specification of customer demands on the contractor. It also needs to set out the responsibilities of the customer for making the partnership work. This is to be welcomed from a security perspective, as it helps to formalize and guarantee the commitment of the customer organization to contribute to essential security processes. It is useful to set out a list of appropriate customer responsibilities for security at a suitable point in the contract, to ensure that such requirements do not get overlooked. Typical commitments might include the following customer responsibilities:

- ensuring that users and their managers are aware of the agreed security rules and responsibilities for the use of the services delivered by the contractor;
- notifying the contractor of changes in security policies, responsibilities, compliance requirements or management processes in sufficient time to plan and implement appropriate changes;
- providing appropriate information and access to enable the contractor to carry out security reviews or risk assessments of new systems;
- notifying the outsourcer when access rights by users need to be changed or are no longer required;
- cooperating with authorized security investigations carried out by the contractor;
- responding to system misuse or access violations detected by the contractor;
- providing the contractor with reasonable notice of security reviews, investigations, audits or tests.

7.8 Avoiding common legal pitfalls

This book is not intended to be a source of legal advice on IT contracts, but it is certainly relevant in the context of outsourcing to mention some of the common legal pitfalls when information systems are delivered by an external service provider. I asked a friend of mine, Dai Davis, a technology lawyer specializing in IT contracts and law, for advice on this issue. Dai maintains a 'top ten' list of common legal pitfalls when negotiating contracts for outsourced application services. Although this list is not intended to be comprehensive, it provides a useful checklist when drawing up commercial contracts.

1) Change of software/data owner

The software used to deliver the services delivered will invariably be licensed. Depending upon the precise business model, the software may be licensed to the vendor or to the customer. In both cases, but especially the latter, it is important to ensure that the licensee is not charged an unreasonable amount when there is a change in customer circumstances, for example when the customer is acquired or merges with another company. The easiest solution is to ensure that the original licence is not terminable on such occurrences.

2) Annual fee renewal

Some licences and maintenance costs are renewed on an annual basis. Often, the fees for future years are not specified or capped by any kind of formula, such as the Retail Price Index, so the licensor will be free to determine the charges for future years. The customer should always aim to establish some degree of certainty about the price of future maintenance and support throughout the lifetime of the contact.

3) Limitations of liability

Limitations of liability are a complex legal subject. The vendor will clearly not wish to accept unlimited liability, as the potential losses in the case of a major failure in services might exceed the value of the contract. At the same time, the customer will be heavily reliant on the vendor's services to maintain critical business processes. Resolving this dichotomy requires the negotiation skills of an experienced lawyer. Ultimately, what can be successfully excluded in law often depends upon a 'reasonableness' test, though some losses, such as personal injury arising though negligence, cannot be excluded or limited.

4) Force majeure

'Force majeure' is a French term which has found its way into many commercial contracts. It can be used to enable a party to avoid its contractual obligations for reasons beyond its control, such as fire, earthquake or shortages of supplies. The vendor will naturally provide generous provisions in his favour. Do not be fooled: the major obligations are on the vendor and it will be the vendor who benefits from this clause, not the customer.

5) Contract termination

It is important to consider the implications of termination at the outset, since the customer will be dependent on the supplier but have limited bargaining power at the time of termination. Key questions to ask are: How long will it take to find another vendor? Will access to the data be possible in order to transfer the data from one vendor to another? Suitable provisions will need to be included in the contract. This subject is covered in more detail in Chapter 9.

6) Change control

Customer requirements are likely to change over time, so it's important to ensure that the prices charged for additions to services will not be unreasonably high. The contract might include anticipated changes with an agreed formula for charges. It will also need to deal with unforeseen additional services by providing a mechanism for quotations. Ultimately, there are only three ways of determining the additional charge for the additional service: the vendor sets the price, the customer sets the price, or an independent expert or mediator decides the price. While the first two options can be expressed in terms of 'reasonableness', both options are invariably unacceptable. The solution is to word the contract in such a way that the option of going to an independent party, although available, is unlikely to be used in practice.

7) Continuity of services
How financially secure is the vendor? The success or survival of the customer organization might depend upon the continuity of the services being provided by the vendor. Default of the vendor will have a serious business impact, but there is little satisfaction in being able to penalize a vendor for non performance if they are declared bankrupt. It is better to avoid contracts with vendors with questionable financial viability than to end up with an expensive failure.

8) Inclusive costs
Are costs inclusive of all extras? It is important to check precisely what is included in the deal, and what is excluded. Some vendors have cost structures which include a charge for each page printed, an overhead which quickly mounts up. Likewise other infrastructure costs, such as telephones, server rental charges and media storage costs might be charged at additional rates. All potential costs need to be established in advance to avoid unpleasant surprises.

9) Foreign suppliers
Offshore services present a range of additional risks, such as lack of immediate control, difference in professional standards and unfamiliarity with English. It is important to balance the price gain that can be achieved by using a foreign vendor against these additional risks. The issues associated with managing a partnership across different cultures are covered in Chapter 9.

10) Data protection
The service provider will have access to, and a degree of control over, the customer's data. If that includes personal data, then both the vendor and the customer will need to register and comply with data protection legislation. UK law now requires that the customer has a written contract with the vendor.

7.9 Learning points from this chapter

This chapter has explored the security issues and requirements for developing and negotiation the outsourcing contract and supporting schedules. Key learning points to note can be summarized as follows.

▶ The contract specifies demands and expectations for the lifetime of the partnership. Further changes will be subject to negotiation and are likely to be expensive to introduce. The contract sets the tone for the ensuing relationship. A prescriptive contract will encourage a formal, less flexible response to service delivery. A more general contract can encourage a more innovative, interactive partnership. Drafting the contract merits close attention to detail and the assignment of the best available advice and resources.

▶ A good contract will clearly specify the services required, how they will be delivered, and who will be responsible for delivering them. It should also define the processes to manage changes, rectify non-compliant deliverables, and resolve disputes. It should be comprehensive and unambiguous, yet adaptable to future changes.

▶ Contract negotiations need strong input from business managers and functional experts. They should not be left in the hands of commercial and legal specialists. The most effective approach is to first get business stakeholders and subject matter experts to define and agree the requirements, and then allow the lawyers to apply the necessary legal and commercial touches.

▶ Typical steps in an ideal process might include
  • developing a business-focused strategy,
  • agreeing a process and timetable with the outsourcer,
  • identifying, arranging and briefing specialist support and subject matter experts,
  • assigning lawyers to draft the main contract, and experts to draft the supporting schedules,
  • checking, improving and agreeing documents before sending to the outsourcer,
  • negotiating and agreeing the draft contact with the outsourcer, and
  • finalizing and approving the contract and schedules.

▶ Contract negotiation should not be a combative process, but it's essential to safeguard the organization's interests and aim for the best deal, though this should not be against the interests of the overall partnership.

▶ Negotiators can employ a range of strategies and tactics, but planning, diplomacy and patience are the real secrets to achieving the best possible outcome. Negotiation strategy is shaped by corporate culture, empowerment, bargaining room, personality and constraints on time, money and resources. Contracts are generally best negotiated in an open, honest fashion, but specific points might need to be negotiated in a firmer, more competitive manner.

▶ Negotiation preferences vary across countries and cultures, and according to personality. Some people avoid conflict, some prefer to compromise, and others like to compete or solve problems. Negotiating tactics might include the exploitation of emotions or deliberately conceding minor issues to leverage for more important concessions. Some tactics aim to wear down the other party, but patience and quiet determination are the most effective qualities.

▶ Discussions should be open, honest and creative, and aim to create advantages for both parties. An adversarial approach is bad for the future relationship and the quality of services delivered. Security is a subject that responds well to creative negotiations that aim to satisfy the interests of both sides. Mutual trust and confidence are the foundations of a successful security relationship.

▶ Ensuring the confidentiality of sensitive data across an outsourced supply chain is a difficult task that should never be underestimated. Security policies, standards and contracts are not enough, and will need to be reinforced by education, vigilance and audit.

▶ The contract will need to accommodate future changes in response to new security requirements. Defined processes should be agreed for the review and refreshment of policies, standards and controls. Security will also need to be maintained through organizational changes, including location changes and subcontracts. The termination of a contract or exit from an outsourcing arrangement will also need to be negotiated. Chapter 11 addresses this subject in more detail.

▶ Excessively detailed specifications will be a constraint on agility. Contracts should aim to be comprehensive and unambiguous, but not overly prescriptive (though this might be appropriate for short-term, offshore contracts). The use of codes of practice and risk assessment methods will help avoid prescriptive specifications.

▶ The contract security schedule defines the security measures that the vendor must implement. It will need to cover general control requirements, for example those based on BS ISO/IEC 27002, *Information technology – Security techniques – Codes of practice for information security management* as well as any specific security requirements to safeguard particular assets from identified risks. The contract should require that existing security requirements are maintained, unless alternative measures have been agreed. The contract should also ensure that outstanding audit actions are addressed and that an annual security improvement plan is agreed to correct legacy weaknesses.

▶ The contractor should be required to demonstrate, at least annually, that the customer's security requirements are being comprehensively applied. The customer should also retain the right to conduct audits, reviews and 'penetration' tests. These are best done through agreed codes of practice to minimize the potential for excessive intrusions or non-cooperation.

▶ Not all requirements fall to the contractor. There are many customer responsibilities that will need to be defined, agreed and taken into account when designing organization and governance processes.

8 Implementing the new arrangement

8.1 Planning considerations

Regardless of the nature of the processes, systems or services that are to be outsourced or offshored, one thing that will always remain in-house is accountability for ensuring their legality, compliance and security. Essential business and security governance processes such as planning, policy, risk management, incident response, business continuity planning, compliance and audit, will need to be re-engineered or adapted to operate across the new partnership.

The outsourcer will probably already operate a similar set of governance processes, but they will almost certainly employ different methods, processes and metrics. New or changed processes and interfaces will therefore have to be established. Business continuity plans, for example, will need to be adapted to accommodate changes in responsibilities and in the nature and location of the platforms used to deliver services, as well as the arrangements for conducting reviews of supply chains and tests of contingency plans.

The need for regular access to the contractor's staff and premises to satisfy security and audit requirements will have to be carefully negotiated, as professional service managers will naturally wish to avoid unnecessary visits or unscheduled interruptions that might have an impact on customer service levels. Both sides will need to sit down, negotiate and agree the frequency and extent of inspections and meetings.

The starting point for the customer will generally be to ask for immediate and constant access to the outsourcer's premises and staff for any form of audit or security investigation. Unfortunately, the starting point for the outsourcer will most likely be to deny any access at all times, without agreement and a generous notice period. The vendor will understandably claim that unscheduled visits will interfere with service delivery and potentially invalidate existing service level agreements. The solution will be a compromise, restricted to an agreed number of audits of specific scopes each year, with appropriate approval processes, notice periods and codes of conduct.

Implementing the new arrangement

When considering implementation planning and execution, key questions to ask are:

- Is there a clear definition of the starting point and the security 'baseline' for the implementation, or must further work be performed, and if so by whom?
- Are there any transitional areas of risk that need special attention prior to or immediately following implementation, e.g. before or after staff are transferred from the customer to the contractor?
- How will the security of interconnections between the customer and contractor be implemented and assured?
- At what point will the security policies, standards and processes that are necessary for the extension of the IT infrastructure to the contractor be in place?
- How will routine audits and reviews be performed, as well as exceptional, ad hoc investigations?

Planning the implementation of an outsourcing contract is more difficult than it appears at first sight. It might sound like a relatively straightforward task to switch the management of a defined set of systems and resources to a new custodian, but in practice it is far from easy. There are many individual security tasks that will have to be carried out to enable and support the transition to the new management. Some are quite time-consuming and will require additional resources to be assigned during this transition period. These activities will need to be identified and taken account of before determining a practical implementation date. Many of these tasks, unfortunately, are not immediately obvious.

An important requirement, which is often overlooked, is the need to destroy all outdated sensitive personal and corporate data from systems, databases and infrastructure that will be handed to the outsourcer. Identifying such data is a major activity, but it can also serve to inform both parties on the processes and systems that generate or handle sensitive data.

A further challenging security activity for contracts involving a bulk transfer of staff is the need to change office passes and access rights for a relatively large number of staff in a very short space of time. Most administrative processes are designed to accommodate a steady trickle of new entrants rather than a bulk transfer of personnel. Bottlenecks such as limited equipment to photograph transition staff and print new identity passes, or limited trained administrators to change access rights, can result in substantial delays in issuing new passes and rights.

It will also be necessary in many cases to develop, agree and implement a secure network design to ensure secure communications and safe network connections between each party's premises and infrastructure. The design will need to take account of considerations such as the level of access required, the security risks introduced by the connection, the security of the infrastructure at each end, the network protocols to be used, the technical solutions available and the performance requirements of the connection.

The design will need to specify the technology needed to meet these requirements, the filtering policies needed to restrict the connectivity and content of the link, and any other technical or physical security controls and constraints required to minimize the resultant security risks. This might have to be implemented in stages because of the lead time to install equipment and configure services.

Even more significant, however, for the longer term, is the impact on governance processes such as risk management, business continuity and regulatory compliance. The organization might be fully compliant before the transition but will be forced to build new processes and to establish fresh compliance assurances from a supplier who might initially be reluctant to admit areas of potential exposure or non-compliance, in case they are seen as a service level failure or a potential liability. New business continuity and crisis arrangements will also have to be agreed and implemented during the transition period. They will need to be maintained at a heightened state of readiness during the initial changeover, as mistakes will inevitably occur following any process involving the transfer of staff, systems or locations.

Disclosure and reporting of information will also need to be strictly controlled. This will be a challenge in an environment of changing responsibilities and reporting lines, in which it is likely that a small percentage of disgruntled staff might wish to express negative opinions that might not be in the best interests of either organization.

Codes of practice, whether drawn up from scratch or adapted from International Standards or previous contracts, are a useful basis for defining and agreeing mutual expectations. They can be used to define and agree essential cooperative governance processes such as risk management, business continuity and audit requirements which will need to be harmonized across the partnership, but might be implemented in a slightly different way. Codes of practice are a non-prescriptive form of standard that can be readily adapted to suit different environments. In the context of an outsourcing contract, such agreements are sometimes referred to as operational level agreements.

There is often an assumption that staff being outsourced or made redundant might be more tempted to commit acts of fraud or sabotage. In fact, nothing could be further from the truth. Certainly some people will be angry, and one or two might even blow their top and vent their anger on the nearest target. But most people losing their jobs or moving to a new organization will generally be on their best behaviour, to ensure their future employment prospects, pension rights and references are adequately safeguarded.

Contingency plans, however, should always take account of the worst possible scenario, so it might be prudent to arrange for enhanced supervision or monitoring of critical activities and events, in order to ensure that any abuse of inside knowledge or privileges by disgruntled staff or former employees is identified and mitigated at the earliest possible opportunity.

8.2 Critical success factors for security governance

Governance is the structure through which the activities of organizations are directed and controlled. It is concerned with the methods and mechanisms applied to set business objectives, control activities and measure performance. Responsibility for governance of the enterprise ultimately lies with the chief executive, but a structure of relationships and processes is generally implemented to communicate business objectives, control requirements and management information across the value chain.

In practice this involves establishing many different roles and processes, including policies, accountabilities, organizational structures, working methods, decision processes, audit mechanisms and reporting systems. Numerous management models and control frameworks have been designed to help organizations implement governance structures in a consistent and auditable way.

In the security field, the most important control framework is the International Standard BS ISO/IEC 27002, *Information technology – Security techniques – Codes of practice for information security management*, which has the advantage of being a certifiable standard. In the IT management field, the most widely used control framework is Control Objectives for Information and Related Technology (COBIT), which is based on 34 high-level processes that cover hundreds of control objectives. This is a large amount of detail to absorb, but, like BS ISO/IEC 27002, the standard is well presented and relatively easy to navigate.

These systems can be helpful to draw on when designing new governance structures, but at the same time they can also introduce a heavy degree of bureaucracy and overheads if followed to the exact letter. Smart governance is about identifying the most effective balance between anarchy and excessive control, one which enables an organization to maintain control of business direction, production and products, to meet legal and compliance obligations and to safeguard shareholder interests, without killing off innovation and smothering the organization in a blanket of excessive rules, controls and paperwork.

This balance is especially important to get right when dealing with outsourced supply chains, where a heavy hand will be unwelcome and in many cases unenforceable, except at prohibitive cost. In particular, it is important not to get so engrossed in the detail that critical success factors are overlooked. In practice, good security governance flows from personal attention to a small number of key factors. These include

- top management commitment: the level of understanding, engagement and *visible* senior-level support for security,
- awareness of information risks, which requires reliable information for decision makers on the nature, probability and impact of security risks,
- professional competence: the degree of professional knowledge, skill and experience available to support risk assessments and decisions on countermeasures,
- benchmarking of the cost of security and how it compares to the value of the benefits delivered and the spending levels of other similar organizations, and
- visibility of security incidents and events: including the availability of current and historical incident data to identify problem areas and prioritize remedial action.

Surprisingly, these are areas that rarely receive the attention they deserve in outsourcing and offshoring contract, but they represent some of the key measures that underpin the success of any major business activity or change initiative. They deserve to be singled out for special attention.

8.3 The Deming Cycle

Plan, Do, Check, Act (PDCA) is a well-established quality-assurance process, also referred to as the 'Deming Cycle' after the distinguished author and management consultant. This cycle, which is illustrated in Figure 7, deserves a special mention

Figure 7 – The Deming Cycle of Plan, Do, Check, Act

as it is now well embedded within many management standards, including information security standards such as BS ISO/IEC 27001. It is designed to achieve continuous improvement of information security management.

The components of a security interpretation of the Deming Cycle are as follows:

Plan: establish the objectives and processes necessary to deliver results in accordance with the organization's security policy.
Do: implement the processes.
Check: monitor and measure processes against security policy, objectives, targets and legal and other requirements, and report results.
Act: take actions to continually improve performance of the security management system.

The Deming Cycle might seem like an obvious, logical approach to security governance, but for many years few organizations took the trouble to 'close the loop' and to check and correct the implementation of security policies and standards. It is only the pressure of regulatory compliance and the growing demand by large customers for accredited certification that has begun to popularize this essential requirement.

The Deming Cycle is also an important enabler for achieving higher levels of process maturity which demand a cycle of continuous improvement. Long-term improvements in any process cannot be achieved by a single, one-off programme of plans and actions. This demands the establishment of a learning process that monitors and measures actual progress against initial objectives and identifies areas requiring remedial action and opportunities for further improvement.

There are many ways of implementing such a feedback loop, but the most effective and efficient method is through the use of accredited certification against an established public standard such as BS ISO/IEC 27000. Accredited certification is an objective, repeatable and regular process performed by qualified, independent auditors, operating to a code of practice.

The advantage to an outsourcer is that it is a process the company can control and schedule at their convenience. It is especially useful where infrastructure is shared by many different customers, as it reduces the amount of time wasted on being repeatedly audited by numerous auditors, using different questionnaires and checklists. With accredited certification a set of systems, infrastructure or an organizational unit can be audited once (regularly) and a certificate provided for the benefit of all customers. At the same time, accredited certification is beneficial to the customers as it substantially reduces the amount of time and money spent on security reviews and internal and external audits.

There is a widespread perception that accredited certification is an expensive process. In fact, the opposite can be true in practice. Accredited certification is an efficient process, based on a defined standard and a well-established methodology. It should be quicker and cheaper than employing in-house staff or expensive security consultants to conduct a less prescriptive security review, such as an SAS 70 audit against a proprietary set of standards, which will involve a greater learning curve and require a much broader range of judgement.

The downside of any accredited certification process, however, is that the results tend to be based more on a 'tick box' exercise than on a considered, professional judgement. A further issue is that the skills, experience and quality of auditors can vary widely, especially across countries. It is important therefore to look for a strong, reliable brand name when assessing the reliability of a certificate.

Organizations need to plan for the fact that any frequent review process is a highly disciplined process, rather like a treadmill in practice. Many managers perceive the implementation of a security management system as a time-boxed exercise, with a degree of subsequent fine tuning. The reality is quite different, with preparation for each subsequent audit becoming progressively more demanding as outstanding audit actions mount up and compete for attention with day-to-day business operations.

8.4 Risk management

Risk management is an essential corporate governance requirement, as well as a fundamental security requirement. It involves the identification, evaluation, prioritization, mitigation, control and monitoring of individual risks to business interests. An example of how to conduct a risk assessment is given in Chapter 2, as part of the planning process for outsourcing.

Most organizations now operate a formal system of risk management process across business units, usually through a network of nominated risk managers in business units supported by a central corporate centre risk management coordination function. Systems and services that are outsourced will be under the control of a different custodian, but the business impact and the responsibility associated with the security risks will remain with the customer, who will therefore need to maintain an effective, agreed process for their assessment and mitigation.

During the transition period, both parties will need to examine their respective processes for security risk management, and to use reasonable endeavours to harmonize or interface their processes. This should be a condition of the contract, but the actual process will need to be developed, agreed and implemented in detail during the transition period following the signing of the contract but before the changeover to the new arrangement.

It is no trivial task to interface and synchronize the activities of risk managers operating across a virtual supply chain. It demands an understanding of the respective methods, reports and schedules used by all parties for assessing risks. These systems might not be compatible because of differences in criteria, scope, scales, weightings and timings.

Where a supplier is primarily delivering a dedicated service to a single customer, it will make sense to aim for a joint approach to risk assessments, perhaps through periodic workshops, in which risks can be identified, evaluated and assigned to an appropriate 'owner' who can take the lead in further defining, mitigating and monitoring each assigned risk. But this might not be feasible in situations where services are shared by many other customers.

Regardless of the circumstances, however, there will be a need for a degree of compromise, standardization and change by all parties. If the contractor does not currently operate a formal risk management process, they should be required by the contract to implement and maintain one, at least for the services to be delivered to the customer. They should also be required to harmonize or interface this process with that of the customer within an agreed time period. The minimum requirement should be to identify, assess and inform the customer on a regular basis, monthly or at least quarterly, of all major risks associated with delivering the specified services, with appropriate advice on the status of each risk and the mitigating actions required.

During the transition stage, both parties will need to draw up an implementation plan, perhaps in stages, to ensure an effective changeover from the existing systems to the new risk management arrangements. The detailed customer requirements and the agreed actions and arrangements to satisfy them should be set out in an agreed code of practice to provide authoritative but adaptable guidance on requirements and expectations to inform future managers. International Standards, such as BS ISO 31000, *Risk management – Principles and guidelines* and BS ISO/IEC 27005 *Information technology – Security techniques – Information security risk management*, can provide a useful reference and input to this code of practice.

8.5 Business continuity

Business continuity management is an essential and well-established management process for identifying potential threats to an organization's critical business processes and developing plans and controls to help mitigate the resulting impact on business operations. It is generally implemented through a framework of individual contingency plans, risk-management measures and incident response processes.

The scope of activities and actions can be very broad, involving preventative measures, detailed plans, fallback arrangements, crisis structures, testing schedules, training courses and crisis exercises. Many of these will be impacted by outsourcing, requiring a major review of overall business continuity strategy, risk profiles, documentation, arrangements and responsibilities.

Professional outsourcers are likely to have a comprehensive set of fallback arrangements and documented disaster recovery plans. These are more than likely to comfortably meet a single customer's contingency requirements, although there might well be opportunities for improvements in business-risk profiles, service availability and recovery-time objectives. The customer will need to ensure, however, that the service provider has appropriate measures, resources and capacity to support simultaneous invocations of disaster plans by several customer organizations, for example, in the event of a widespread regional or national disaster.

The starting point should therefore be to review business continuity strategy, taking account of both the capabilities and limitations introduced by the contractor, before identifying the need for changes to existing plans, processes and responsibilities. Individual documents outlining responsibilities and actions will then need to be updated with new names and contact details. It is a good idea to arrange for an early crisis exercise and test of fallback arrangements, which should form part of an agreed schedule of periodic exercises and tests.

8.6 Audit rights

Regular audits and reviews of service providers are essential for customers, but they also are potentially disruptive to service providers, who will naturally seek to avoid interruptions which might, among other things, impact customer service levels. The audit schedule to the contract should therefore clearly define what comprises an audit, as well as how many such audits or reviews each year are reasonable, how much notice is required and what level of cooperation is reasonable to expect.

It is especially important to define the range of audit information that should be made available, such as records, accounts, books, data, documents and other information that might be relevant to the performance of the services, or necessary to demonstrate compliance with contractual obligations. Such access cannot extend to all information. For example, it should encompass records of time spent by the contractor's staff on customer projects, but it need not extend to specific details of an employee's actual pay. The customer, however, will also need to undertake not to disclose any confidential information obtained through audits or security reviews or investigations.

The range of audits that will be needed is likely to be quite extensive and it is important to ensure that categories of essential audits or reviews are not overlooked when drawing up a list of permissible audit themes and objectives. Each organization will, of course, have its own specific demands for audits, but a typical range of audit subjects might include the following activities:

- internal and external audits;
- project-management activities;
- risk-management processes;
- business continuity and disaster recovery;
- corporate governance and compliance requirements;
- security reviews (including confidentiality, integrity and availability) of services and data;
- security investigations;
- penetration testing and security vulnerability assessments;

- processes concerned with the provision of management information;
- compliance with legal and regulatory compliance requirements;
- financial processes, including accounting, calculation of charges and pricing structures;
- data protection and privacy;
- legal investigations, reviews and discovery actions;
- benchmarking exercises.

Clearly, such a list represents a large number of potential disruptions for a service provider. It will therefore need to be strictly controlled with agreed limits on the number of audits and a defined authorization processes to help prioritize the need for audits. A further issue is to determine *who* might be authorized to carry out an audit or review. Clearly the contractor would wish to avoid the use of any company they regard as a major competitor. This thinking might rule out, for example, many top audit companies ranked by leading analysts such as Gartner, as potential competitors in the same market.

The customer, however, will seek and expect the maximum choice of candidates. This could include auditors who might not represent a direct competitive threat, but could well be judged by an independent authority to be operating in the same competitive market. The most appropriate compromise for such a situation is to agree a list of approved auditors or reviewers prior to signing the contract. This list might include, for example, many respected independent companies who operate in similar markets to the contractor but are not regarded as a source of competition. Such a pragmatic approach can help to ensure a maximum choice of auditors, while at the same time neatly sidestepping the issue of failing to agree on an approved audit organization.

These agreed arrangements should be set out in an agreed code of practice, setting out minimum requirements and expectations, but in a flexible way that enables pragmatic interpretations to solve day-to-day business issues. The code of practice should establish the rights and limits of the customer or its external auditors and agents to audit any activity relating to the services delivered, unless this might infringe obligations of confidentiality, for example owed by the contractor to another client.

The customer should also aim to reserve the right to perform quality checks of deliverables against agreed specifications. The audit schedule and associated code of practice should clearly set out the entitlements and obligations of the customer, including

- the number of full, formal audits that might be undertaken each year,
- the limit of ad hoc, selective audits that might be needed to meet specific corporate policies or regulatory compliance requirements,
- responsibilities for approving, arranging and scheduling audit interviews or inspections,
- the required notice period for requesting meetings, interviews or visits,
- the degree of access that can be reasonably expected to people, buildings, information or systems,
- who is authorized to carry out audits, inspections, reviews and investigations, and
- business hours during which audits can take place.

It is also prudent to arrange a special exemption for urgent investigations, for example involving fraud or criminal activity, where, subject to an agreed authorization process, immediate access to buildings, records and personnel might be needed. On completion of every audit, the customer should be required to inform the contractor of findings and recommendations, and to gain the service provider's agreement for, and commitment to, relevant remedial actions and improvements.

A further essential requirement to support audits is the need, which should be a condition of the contract, for the contractor to maintain full, true and accurate records of accounts, books, data, records, documents, equipment and other information that is either relevant to the services provided or needed to meet legal or regulatory compliance requirements. Such information will also need to be safeguarded from potential loss, destruction or modification.

Auditors and security managers should be at their highest state of alert during the changeover to the new management systems. It is worth considering incorporating temporary, additional, monitoring processes and controls to ensure that problems, mistakes and oversights are spotted at the earliest possible stage, well before the maximum business damage can be caused. Such controls can then be progressively withdrawn as confidence builds in the new arrangements.

8.7 Security investigations

Security investigations present a similar, but slightly different issue to audits. They can be intrusive and disruptive for the contractor, but far less predictable.

In a bad year they might demand frequent access to the contractor's facilities and staff, yet in a good year require virtually no intrusions at all.

A further difference is that the range of customer staff that will require access to support security investigations is considerably smaller than that needed for audits and reviews. The arrangements for security investigations are, therefore, best developed and negotiated separately from those for general audits and reviews. Such arrangements will need to consider a different set of issues and requirements such as the following, which should be set out in an agreed code of practice for the conduct of security investigations.

- Who on the customer side is authorized to submit a request for an investigation, and who on the contractor side will be responsible for approving it?
- How quickly will the request need to be approved, and access to premises and information granted?
- What are the identification requirements for investigators requiring access to the contractor's premises?
- What special training or qualifications are needed by investigators in order to be given access to equipment or software?
- What levels of access and support are reasonable to expect to support particular types of investigation?
- What are the confidentiality requirements, including the need to comply with legal or compliance requirements?
- What are the approval and arrangement procedures for removal of equipment for inspection or evidence, especially where this might impact service levels?

The contract should address potential issues, such as liabilities and claims, arising from a security incident and the subsequent investigation.

8.8 Learning points from this chapter

This chapter has explored the considerations and activities involved in implementing a new outsourcing arrangement. Key learning points to note can be summarized as follows.

▶ Regardless of the nature of the services to be outsourced or offshored, accountability for ensuring their legality, compliance and security will remain in-house. Critical success factors for good security governance include top management commitment, awareness of information risks, professional competence, benchmarking of costs, and visibility of security incidents and events.

▶ Many individual security tasks will need to be carried out to support the transition to the new arrangement, for example the need to destroy outdated data from systems, to change office passes and access rights, and to implement a secure network design between each party's premises and infrastructure. Disclosure and reporting of information will also need to be strictly controlled.

▶ Staff transitioning to the new organization or being made redundant will generally be on their best behaviour to safeguard their future employment prospects, pension rights and references, but contingency plans should be drawn up to take account of worst-case scenarios.

▶ Each party will have their own governance processes but might employ different methods and measures. During the transition period, both parties will need to examine their respective processes for risk management and business continuity, and apply reasonable endeavours to harmonize or interface them. It is a good idea to arrange for an early crisis exercise and test of fallback arrangements.

▶ The design of new governance processes should draw on established standards such as BS ISO/IEC 27002, *Information technology – Security techniques – Codes of practice for information security management* and COBIT, but aim to avoid excessive bureaucracy and overheads. Codes of practice are a useful basis for defining and agreeing mutual expectations, as they can be interpreted and adapted to suit the circumstances of each party.

▶ The Deming Cycle – 'Plan, Do, Check, Act', – is a well-established quality assurance process, which is embedded in many management standards. It is designed to achieve continuous improvement of information security management, and so is an important enabler for achieving higher levels of process maturity.

▶ The use of independent accredited certification can enable the outsourcer to maintain a degree of control of the assurance process. It should be encouraged, but it is important to look for a reliable brand name when assessing the reliability of a certificate.

▶ An excessive number of audits can impact service levels, so both parties will need to agree on a set of rules and procedures. The range of audits required can be extensive and will need to be agreed in advance to avoid the risk of non-cooperation. The contractor will wish to avoid the use of any audit companies they regard as competitors. Special arrangements will be needed for urgent security investigations involving fraud or criminal activity, where immediate access to buildings, records and personnel might be needed.

▶ Auditors and security managers should be at their highest state of alert during the changeover to the new management systems. Temporary additional monitoring processes and controls might be needed to ensure that problems are spotted at the earliest possible stage, before major business damage can be caused.

9 Managing the relationship

9.1 Building a successful relationship

A good working relationship is vital to the success of the partnership. Effective security management relies on continuous visibility and reporting of events, as well as close cooperation in managing day-to-day risks and incidents. Management of the relationship, however, should not be left solely to the best efforts of individuals. To be effective, it requires a proactive strategy. In particular, organizational interests will need to be aligned on both sides of the partnership in order to create a win/win outcome, rather than allowing a potential win/lose approach to decision-making to develop.

The relationship will generally be at its healthiest immediately prior to the award of contract, when the customer and supplier are both keen to close a deal and therefore willing to cooperate. But it is likely to become more formal, distant and defensive once the contract is signed. Strong leadership is important to set the right tone and engagement style for the relationship. The most productive partnerships are those in which all parties work together as a single, virtual team, although this is harder than it might sound to achieve in practice, as it demands a level of maturity on both sides that rarely develops until much later in the life of the contract. It is also important to plan to manage the performance of the relationship, and to both provide and obtain the objective evidence needed to encourage continuous improvement.

When considering relationship management, key questions to ask are:

- What mechanisms and processes need to be put in place to allow the relationship to succeed?
- What factors might cause the relationship to turn sour? For example, would it be a failure of performance, an overambitious expectation, or a subjective perception?
- If the relationship turns sour, how will each side escalate the issue? Will they, for example, immediately refer the issue to legal advisors, or will operational managers have the means to resolve dispute?
- What positive steps can be taken proactively to improve the relationship, rather than just aiming to prevent it from getting worse?

The contract should contain simple, basic mechanisms to encourage a good relationship. Examples of this might be regular meetings, assigned relationship managers, escalation procedures, exchanges of personnel, and incentives to identify and implement improvements. A good contract will help to promote a healthy, positive relationship.

Clear commercial incentives for the contractor, for example, will help to attract the pick of the outsourcer's staff to the partnership, and generally encourage a quality response to new business requirements. In contrast, a contract that offers few longer-term incentives to the service provider can create a climate of pessimism, stifling innovation and discouraging good staff from being assigned to, or attracted to, the contract.

The need to attract and retain the best available contractor's staff is important, as employees in an outsourcing services organization are often relatively mobile across customer contracts, and many services operate a form of in-house market, where the best staff will be offered to the most valuable contracts. In practice, it is unrealistic for a customer to aim to prevent a supplier from substituting staff. Buyers rarely get more than what they pay for. If the business objective is to achieve the lowest costs then the customer should not expect to retain the best staff. The most effective solution will be to ensure that performance measures embedded in the contract are sufficiently detailed to capture the quality of the outputs, rather than the quality of the inputs and resources used to create those outputs.

It is important also to forge relationships with the right people at the right level in the contractor's organization. Managing security issues at the wrong level or with the wrong person can be frustrating by raising customer expectations that cannot easily be fulfilled. Attempting to maintain multiple relationships can be equally problematic, as it will become excessively time-consuming for both sides, and it can create communication problems. Security managers on the customer side should aim to identify a suitable security focal point in the contractor's organization at an appropriate level: one that is close enough to day-to-day activities to be reasonably informed about operational events and risks, and yet sufficiently senior to make decisions and drive through major changes.

Key relationships should be identified and established from the start, and an appropriate schedule of meetings agreed, ideally weekly but at the very least monthly. Useful communications channels should also be maintained through commercial account managers, who have a broader perspective on general decisions, developments and relationships associated with the contract. Managing outsourced services demands much broader skills than those needed to manage in-house technology projects. Sound technical knowledge and project management expertise are a good start, but they will not guarantee influence over third-party decision-making.

In theory, security managers should be comfortable in dealing with third-party organizations. In the security world, many practitioners live on their contacts, depending on external security and law enforcement agencies, as well as their own counterparts in other organizations, for intelligence and best practices. They are generally better networked than other IT professionals, and more inclined to develop deeper, trusted relationships in order to share privileged knowledge about recent incidents and emerging security threats. Such skills are crucial in helping to build a trusted partnership that might encourage the contractor's security managers to share confidential information about risks and incidents, and motivate them to apply their very best endeavours to safeguard their customer's security interests.

Security is best approached as a shared set of objectives for the security teams on both sides of the relationship. It is generally in both parties' interests to ensure that major incidents are avoided and that their consequences are rectified speedily. Contractual issues or arguments about who is to blame are highly unproductive points to escalate during a major security incident.

9.2 Relationship management

Relationship management is a well-understood and long-practised art. Diplomats, salesmen and commercial brokers have been exploiting it for thousands of years, and advice can also be sought from many internal and external professionals who are to be found operating in these roles, for example in legal, HR or commercial functions. There are some well-established principles for building good relationships, which every information security manager should study and apply. They can be equally useful in day-to-day business and personal life, as well as in the more confined constraints of an outsourcing contract.

The most powerful concepts are perhaps the simplest ones. For example, the starting point in developing good relationship management skills is to recognize that when we talk to other people they are generally less interested in our challenges, problems and ideas, than they are in their own activities and issues.

Telling them about our skills, strengths and achievements will attract little interest. But asking them about their own interests will create a more positive impression. Such questions can also deliver valuable feedback. Establishing what makes managers tick, and what is occupying their minds and attention, is useful intelligence for any security manager.

Start by asking the contractor's managers to explain how their business works, what problems they currently face, and what targets and ambitions they have set for the future. These questions serve a dual purpose of generating useful insights, as well as demonstrating a level of interest in their work that will help to form a useful bond, and immediately increase the prospects of building a stronger longer-term relationship and gaining their future cooperation.

Personal style and presentation can also make a big difference. Most people respond positively to a pleasant countenance, a polite introduction, a sense of humour and a smile. Threats and criticism are a bad basis for influencing people, as they encourage the recipients to become more defensive and less cooperative. Humour, modesty and self-deprecation can be the most effective tools for gaining friends and influencing other people.

A small amount of background research on individuals can also help to demonstrate an interest in them. Small things such as being able to pronounce a person's name correctly, recognizing their achievements, and remembering their personal details will leave a powerful, positive impression. As Dale Carnegie, author of the classic book *How to win friends and influence people* once put it: 'Remember that a person's name is to that person the sweetest and most important sound in any language.' Listening skills are especially important, both for creating a constructive dialogue and for gaining intelligence on business developments and issues. Unreliable memories can be overcome by keeping notes in a contacts database, though these need to be carefully used and safeguarded in accordance with data protection principles. The results, however, can be highly effective.

9.3 Managing diversity and different cultures

Managing offshore services is a tougher challenge because of the physically remote nature of the relationship, as well as the inevitable differences in culture, management style and outlook. The customer might well be king from a financial perspective, but it is the local employees who determine the ultimate quality and success of the services delivered. Gaining the best response from the contract demands a certain amount of adaptation to local circumstances, culture and practices. This helps to avoid misunderstandings and enable you to get the best results from the local staff.

When managing any offshore contract, it pays dividends to take the trouble to study the history of the country and its customs and religions. Many overseas cultures and communities have different values and priorities to our own. It is easy to unintentionally cause offence, create a misunderstanding or set off a dispute through a misinterpretation of the language or a local custom. Successful managers will aim to recognize and adapt to local differences, rather than seeking to impose their own set of values and practices. Unfortunately, this is not an instinctive skill.

We often naturally assume that other people are similar to us in likes, dislikes and beliefs. The reality is that they can be markedly different. Taking the time and trouble to understand other cultures, their interests, politics and geography, will help you to better understand and resolve operational issues. It will also help to avoid embarrassment through ignorance of local facts and customs. An interest in people and their cultures is educational and it lies at the heart of good diplomacy and relationship management. Respect flows from a healthy interest in individuals and their community. It is far better to understand and manage cultural differences rather than approach these differences as risks.

Far Eastern cultures can have markedly different manners, loyalties, and degrees of formality, openness and empowerment to Western cultures. There are also significant differences in approaches to personal and business networking. Generally speaking, Eastern executives have a preference for building longer-term, trusted commercial partnerships, in contrast to the more open, short-term, competitive approach to business favoured by Western executives. In the East, business partners are often selected on a strategic basis; in the West it is more likely to be on the basis of the best bid received in response to an invitation to tender. Religion and culture will also play a major part in shaping personal priorities, the influence of authority, and the perception of business risks.

Avoiding 'loss of face' is a major concern in many Eastern cultures. Criticism of individuals can create a strong adverse reaction and leave a bad long-term impression. It can also be difficult to get local staff to admit to problems and difficulties. This encourages the so-called 'Mum effect': the reluctance to report negative information.

Questions and demands should be diplomatically phrased to create a good impression and encourage a more positive response. It is better, for example, to challenge local managers to suggest actions for improvement, rather than ask them to admit failings and problems. Regardless of how frustrating it might seem, it is vital to avoid causing managers or colleagues to lose face as this will create a damaging perception of your behaviour, and one that might be extremely hard to counteract, potentially impairing your long-term standing and relationship with the local community.

Loyalty can be a key issue, as the perceived relative importance of company, family and community interests varies across cultures. Hispanic and Asian cultures, for example, generally value family needs above company interests, whereas in many Western communities, loyalty to the company takes precedence. All of these interests should therefore be aligned as far as possible. Hierarchy is also important in many cultures. Respect for maintaining face can discourage subordinates from challenging or correcting their boss. In some cultures there might also be different levels of formality for business meetings, which are important to recognize and respect.

Personal attitudes, humour and behaviour can vary widely across different communities. Many Asians enjoy competitive negotiations but can be easily offended by a display of arrogance or conceit. Adopting a humble attitude is always the best approach. Humour can be a risky tactic. Jokes are generally best avoided, unless they are clearly at your own expense. Patience is required when negotiating with Asian business executives, many of whom attach less importance to time and rarely like to make quick decisions, preferring to focus on longer-term relations rather than immediate deals.

Language differences between cultures are a frequent cause of misunderstandings in offshore contracts. It is therefore essential to confirm, and perhaps re-confirm, that all requests, specifications and instructions have been completely understood. Special attention should be given to English words that do not translate correctly into other languages. Some do not exist, or do not have an equivalent meaning, in other languages.

For example, the word 'no' does not exist in Thai vocabulary. The word 'sisu' is a unique Finnish concept that represents a philosophy that, if something has to be done it will definitely be done, regardless of what it takes. Other words might be translated with a different meaning. The Japanese word 'hai' generally translates as 'yes', but might not signify agreement, depending on the context, which could indicate one of various shades of meaning. For example, if preceded by the question 'Don't you think that …' it will mean 'no'.

Similarly, in some cultures it is common to say 'yes' even when you do not necessarily agree with a request, and have no intention of carrying it out. Hand or body gestures can also be misconstrued. An Asian person might shake their head to indicate interest, but this could easily be interpreted as a sign of disagreement by a Western person. Some cultures use hand gestures to communicate in a way that can completely transform the meaning of their words. They might even be saying they agree with you, but their hands might indicate the opposite.

Even people who share a common language can encounter problems. Western executives speaking English can also misinterpret each other, as some words are used differently. The verb 'bin', for example, can mean 'file' in America but 'junk' in the UK, a potentially dangerous misunderstanding. Globalization, however, is progressively closing many of the gaps in culture, practice and pricing between the major Eastern and Western outsourcers. Both are now proficient in delivering global services, but getting the best out of staff across a range of different locations and cultures will always remain a major challenge.

9.4 Resolving disputes

Outsourcing contracts are generally relatively large, complex, long-term partnerships, compared to most other commercial purchases. It would be surprising if there were no major areas of disagreement or complaint. Disputes should be anticipated, and appropriate arrangements made to contain and resolve them.

Most disputes are best dealt with at the earliest possible stage, before they generate heated arguments, emotional responses, and consequential business damage. The most effective countermeasure in minimizing the number and impact of disputes is to identify and address potential areas of conflict before they arise. Regular service reviews, for example, will help identify problem areas and explore useful opportunities for improvement. Joint planning exercises will also help align business objectives and service expectations on both sides.

In addition, the contract should include a formal, agreed complaints procedure, to ensure there is no ambiguity on what constitutes a complaint or how it will be addressed. The service provider should also establish an efficient process for recording customer complaints and initiating appropriate, remedial action. This process should include a mechanism for jointly reviewing and escalating outstanding complaints to senior management. At the highest level, this might include immediate attention by the CEO of the outsourcing organization.

Maintaining and reviewing statistics of incidents, complaints and corresponding actions can help to highlight trends or issues in resolving incidents. It is important, however, to recognize frequent complaints as potential relationship issues rather than mere statistics on a chart. Customer satisfaction measures can also help to identify potential problem areas that might require more personal attention.

Again, these statistics need to be regarded as leading indicators of emerging issues rather than numbers that need to be explained away. The purpose of customer satisfaction measures should be to resolve issues and improve services, not to generate evidence to support potential contractual claims. When it comes to a major dispute involving legal action, however, statistics gathered over a period of time will carry more weight than anecdotal evidence.

Resolving a major dispute is neither fast nor cheap. For thousands of years people have been striving to resolve disputes in many different walks of life using a variety of methods, sometimes with success, but in many cases with no satisfactory outcome. Experience has taught us that there are two main approaches to resolving disputes. You can either attempt to resolve the problem with your partner through a consensual process such as negotiation, either with or without third-party assistance. Or you can employ an adjudicative process, in which an arbitrator, judge or jury decides the outcome.

Indeed, a large part of the legal system exists primarily to resolve disputes. The fact that there are so many lawyers is testament to the need for independent judgements to resolve many disputes. Negotiation is a powerful tool, but it only works if there are clear incentives for both sides to arrive at an agreed outcome. A key factor, of course, is whether both parties want to resolve the dispute. If one side sees no advantage in changing the status quo then it will prove difficult to agree any form of change. This is often the case when a customer is dissatisfied with the services delivered by a vendor.

In such cases, a formal process will generally be required to persuade the supplier to address the problem. Contracts must therefore include appropriate mechanisms for resolving disputes, including agreed penalties, service credits, escalation processes, and arrangements for professional mediation. At the time of contract negotiation these provisions might appear to be contingency measures to be used in exceptional circumstances, but they can soon become a part of everyday business.

Litigation is the last resort for resolving a dispute. If a dispute reaches this stage then other routes to agreement will have been tried, and failed. Litigation should not be regarded as an achievement or step forward. It represents a formal recognition of a failure of the contracted arrangement.

In such a situation, the outcome is effectively taken out of the hands of the partnership and decided by a third party though an objective, factual process. Evidence will therefore need to be collected and presented to support claims. The resulting decision will be binding, though an appeal might be possible.

In contrast, mediation is a much softer process that aims to find a solution that is acceptable to both parties. Mediation is a form of dispute resolution that assists both parties in negotiating an agreed outcome. It is driven by needs and wants, rather than facts and figures. Both parties negotiate and decide the conditions of the settlement that is reached, rather than being bound by the recommendation of a third party. Mediators are skilled negotiators who aim to enhance the dialogue between the parties in dispute.

Arbitration is a more objective method for resolving disputes outside of the courts. It involves referring the matter to an independent arbitrator, by whose decision both parties agree to be bound.

Techniques that can assist in mediating disputes include the use of a neutral environment and a non-emotional negotiation processes. Physical surroundings can in fact have a major impact on behaviour, an influence that should not be underestimated. Protocols and principles will need to be agreed on in advance, for example the need to consciously avoid immediate criticism of the other party's statements. In fact, the key to constructive negotiation and dispute resolution is to listen carefully and make an effort to understand the perspective of the other side. This not only helps solve the immediate problems, it will also help to build a better relationship for the future.

Prevention is, of course, always cheaper, more effective and more satisfactory than a cure. The best and most natural form of mediation is when both parties aim to anticipate and resolve complaints and differences of opinion before any serious dispute arises. Such a process should be initiated at the earliest stage when a complaint is initially reported.

Good communication, frequent monitoring and honest reporting are the fundamentals of successful dispute prevention. In particular, it's important to encourage a 'no-blame' culture to enable frank exchanges and reporting, rather than a blame culture which seeks primarily to identify scapegoats and, in the process, acts to unnecessarily escalate grievances. Escalation processes should be used sparingly to address serious problems that cannot be resolved through routine dialogues and protocols.

Anecdotal evidence from experienced contract lawyers suggests that more than two thirds of all outsourcing deals are renegotiated within two years of the contract being signed. There are many different reasons for this, but most issues tend to revolve around service pricing, business changes or performance. Security is also a frequent issue that increasingly crops up in partnership disputes, usually because of an incomplete specification, a policy that is open to different interpretations, or a change in the perceived risk profile of an application system or business service.

The problem with security issues is that they are rarely judged to be *material*, and might not therefore be sufficiently significant to initiate or influence the course of a formal escalation process. But following any large outsourcing deal, it is common to find numerous small points of disagreement about how security is managed. This is to be expected, in fact, given that contemporary security standards contain in excess of a hundred individual control descriptions. Indeed, it would be remarkable if such a standard could be interpreted without any issues or differences in interpretation.

Resorting to a legal process to resolve differences of opinion, however, is rarely a realistic option for security issues – for two reasons. The first reason is that, as mentioned above, the issues are unlikely to be substantial enough to trigger immediate legal action. Second, the issues involved would probably take so long to resolve that the business exposure from the disputed control is unlikely to be addressed in real time.

The reality of a contemporary contract is that for each significant security issue, there are likely to be more than 10 times that number of issues relating to other aspects of service delivery. In fact, for a large outsourcing contract there might well be hundreds of issues raised by each side, at any one stage. In such a situation, it is not a reliable strategy to rely on a legal process to resolve these security issues, as they will be lost in a sea of more general complaints. Alternative, quicker means of resolution are best pursued in order to achieve a faster solution that minimizes the business impact of security exposures.

Approaches that can be considered to resolve security disputes include the following.

- Look for commercial incentives for the vendor that can be informally traded in exchange for remedial action.
- Develop a broader solution that might also deliver benefits to the other party.
- Build a closer, trusted relationship, and appeal to the desire of the other party to take action in order to sustain or perhaps even cultivate this relationship.
- Appeal to the professionalism of the contractor's security staff to correct the situation.
- Use the threat of legal action as a catalyst for encouraging immediate action.

Conducting an independent, root cause analysis following a security incident, or when security is cited as a reason for a project failure, cost/schedule overrun or service deterioration, will also help to avoid damaging perceptions that are not consistent with the facts.

9.5 Managing incidents across organizational boundaries

One of the most difficult challenges associated with outsourcing is to develop a capability to manage a major incident, disaster or crisis that encompasses a virtual supply chain. There are several reasons why this scenario is a major challenge.

First, there is the obvious dependency on an outside party to deliver the changes necessary to resolve any problem related to the outsourced services. Second, there is the issue of determining who should actually take the lead. Determining who leads the decision-making might not, at first sight, appear to be a major issue. A customer faced with an impending crisis caused by a major service outage, for example, will naturally feel entitled to call the shots. But they will quickly discover that they are just one of many large customers affected.

In addition, there is the very real risk that any customer organization taking the driving seat is to some extent accepting a degree of liability for crisis judgements. At the same time, customers will find that in a crisis they are significantly disadvantaged and disempowered in their judgements by a lack of

---

visibility, knowledge and technical skills, all of which are needed to assess the situation, determine the most appropriate response, and generally oversee and monitor progress in managing the crisis.

In fact, the essential starting point in establishing an effective crisis response across a partnership is to ensure that each team involved clearly understands the scope, structure, roles, contact details and call-out procedures of the other response teams. This in itself is a major challenge across a new and evolving partnership, which is generally subject to constant changes in organizational structure and assignment of individual roles.

The second fundamental requirement is to determine how best to interface with the partner's team structure. This is rarely a straightforward decision, as there are likely to be substantial differences in the levels, seniority, membership and degree of empowerment of each partner's crisis team arrangements. In particular, it will be necessary to ensure that protocols, escalation processes and working methods remain as consistent as possible across the supply chain.

A particular challenge is to ensure that the timing of crisis conference calls are efficiently synchronized, as team members are likely to be tied up for a considerable amount of time during a crisis in giving instructions, overseeing remedial action, fielding enquiries and briefing senior management, not to mention the time spent in networking with other private or community crisis focal points.

Good crisis team-working demands advance planning and regular exercises, supplemented by considered analysis of identified problems, as well as the development of smart working methods and reliable communications channels. Many practical problems and potential improvements in managing a virtual crisis team arrangement can only be identified through trial and error.

Practice is essential, and will help to bring home the importance of openness and trust between partners. In the early stages of a commercial relationship, for example, there is likely to be a relatively high degree of reticence and secrecy about security events and inside information, especially those items that might imply liability, impact service level agreements, or potentially impact corporate reputation. An effective crisis response, however, cannot be established without an open discussion of the full facts and the potential intelligence surrounding an incident. Such a level of trust can only be achieved over a period of time, as each partner comes to appreciate the benefits of sharing information as much as the consequences of the associated risks.

A further skill that needs to be developed is how best to go about conducting efficient crisis team discussions using conference calls across remote locations, rather than relying on traditional, face-to-face discussion within a physical crisis room.

Conference calls are a difficult medium for fast-moving, collaborative decision-making, especially when the participants do not know each other. Knowledge-sharing and discussions are severely limited by the fact that people take turns to speak and it's not easy to share visual information or convey signs of approval or dissent. Many participants will also be distracted by events in their local environment, such as incoming emails.

New rules, protocols and skills will therefore need to be developed to improve the efficiency of crisis teams operating through conference calls. Again, this points to the need for good planning, preparation and regular exercises to build the skills and best practices for managing fast-moving incidents across virtual supply chains.

9.6 Security improvements

The implementation of information security measures will always lag behind the risks and compliance requirements that demand them. New threats and compliance requirements are constantly emerging, and exposures in legacy systems will periodically come to light. The security of outsourced services will therefore need to be periodically updated.

Rather than leave this to the vagaries of ad hoc negotiations, which are likely to be unreliable and expensive, it is much better to agree an annual security improvement programme, incorporated at an agreed, but variable cost. Such a programme, which will need to be agreed in advance by both parties, should aim to improve the compliance level of legacy systems, or their environment, in order to keep pace with current or emerging security and compliance requirements.

Other tools to consider might include the following:

- a 'lessons learned' process, for example where a security incident has been poorly handled or a development project has suffered schedule/cost overruns after having to apply security retrospectively;
- process and data quality improvement initiatives;
- joint workshops outside the workplace to reflect on recent experiences and engage creatively to identify better ways of working.

9.7 Learning points from this chapter

This chapter has explored the issues and considerations involved in successfully managing the outsourcing relationship. Key learning points to note from this chapter can be summarized as follows.

▶ A good working relationship is vital to effective security management, which relies on reporting of events, and cooperation in managing risks and incidents. Good relationship management demands a proactive strategy that aligns interests on both sides of the partnership to create a win/win outcome.

▶ Relationships are usually good before the award of contract, but can become distant and defensive once the contract is signed. Strong leadership is needed to set the right tone and encourage all parties to work as a single, virtual team. It will also be necessary to manage the performance of the relationship, and collect evidence to support continuous improvement.

▶ Useful mechanisms to encourage a good relationship include regular meetings, assigned relationship managers, escalation procedures, exchanges of personnel, and incentives to identify and implement improvements. Relationships should be forged with the right people at the right level in the contractor's organization, at a point that is close to day-to-day operations but senior enough to drive through changes.

▶ There are well-established principles for building good relationships. The starting point is to take an interest in people. A pleasant, polite style also helps. Threats and criticism encourage recipients to be defensive and uncooperative. Humour, modesty and self-deprecation are effective devices for helping to gain friends and influence people.

▶ Managing offshore contracts is harder, because of cultural differences and restrictions on communications. Many overseas communities have different values and priorities. It is easy to create misunderstandings or cause offence. Taking the trouble to understand the culture will help to avoid and resolve operational issues. Globalization is progressively closing many of the gaps in culture, practice and pricing between Eastern and Western outsourcers, but getting the best out of staff across different locations and cultures remains a major challenge.

▶ Culture, religion, hierarchy and loyalty can all play a major part in shaping staff priorities. Avoiding loss of face is a particular concern in the East, so criticism should be avoided as far as possible. Language differences are a frequent cause of misunderstandings in offshore contracts. Instructions and agreements should be confirmed and re-confirmed. Some commonly used words, such as 'yes' and 'no' might not always translate consistently.

► Disputes are inevitable in any long-term, complex partnerships. They should be anticipated and arrangements made to identify, contain and resolve them. Regular service reviews can help to identify problem areas and opportunities for improvement. Joint planning exercises help align business objectives and expectations. Formal complaints procedures provide reassurances about complaint handling. Statistics of incidents, complaints and actions can help to highlight trends and issues.

► Resolving major disputes through legal action is neither fast nor cheap, and should be avoided if possible. Disputes can be resolved through consensual processes such as negotiation, or by employing an independent arbitrator to decide the outcome. Prevention is better than cure. Both parties should aim to anticipate and resolve complaints or differences of opinion before any serious dispute arises. Good communication and a 'no-blame' culture encourage open exchanges and honest reporting. Conducting an independent, root cause analysis of security incidents will also help to avoid incorrect, damaging perceptions of who or what is to blame.

► Litigation is the last resort for resolving a dispute. It should not be regarded as an achievement, as it represents a failure of the arrangement. It is rarely a realistic option for a security issue, as it will take a long time to resolve. It is better to appeal to the professionalism of the contractor's security staff to correct the situation.

► Managing a major incident across a virtual supply chain is a challenge because of the lack of visibility and potential confusion of roles. Each crisis team needs to understand the scope, structure, roles, contact details and call-out procedures of the other response teams. Good planning, reliable communications and regular exercises are needed.

► New security threats, vulnerabilities and compliance requirements are constantly emerging, requiring the security of the outsourced services to be updated. An annual security improvement programme should be agreed to enable this to be achieved at reasonable cost.

10 Review, termination and exit

10.1 Planning for a major change

Many outsourcing and offshoring arrangements are long-term commitments, often lasting several years perhaps with a single prime contractor. There is, in fact, an interesting current trend for many mature outsourcing customers to aim for shorter contracts based on multiple specialist vendors. But regardless of business strategy, outsourcing will always remain a long-term investment.

The reason for this is simple: the process of switching a portfolio of business services to an external or alternative provider generally takes a long time, typically in excess of a year for a sizeable IT service portfolio. This period might be even longer for applications that are rich in essential proprietary features, which is, for example, a common feature of many cloud-based application services. Whether the customer likes it or not, outsourcing is a process that is difficult and time-consuming to reverse or change. Contracts can be made shorter, but business dependencies and technical constraints will often prevent a quick or painless exit from a contract that turns sour.

The implication of this dependency is that advance planning for a change of service provider will need to commence well in advance of the transfer, and that an appropriate degree of contingency planning will also need to be carried out to cater for the event of a failure or damaging dispute with the outsourcer that might lead to a major impact to critical business services. In addition, it is likely that a number of major changes will be required over the period of the contract: to meet new business requirements, for example, or to take advantage of new technologies, or to respond to changes in the business environment.

Outsourcing contracts require mechanisms for anticipating major changes in business volumes, technologies or market pricing, as well as the need to prepare for a change in outsourcer, as a result, for example, of persistent failures to meet service level targets. The contract should include suitable arrangements for managing major changes, whether in business demand, product pricing, technology, regulatory compliance or business applications, especially those that extend beyond the scope of a routine change control request. In addition, the contract should address the implications of a potential termination of contract.

Review, termination and exit

An exit strategy is a negotiated means of escaping from a potentially unfavourable situation. The contract should include agreements that will enable either party to terminate the contract prior to the agreed end date. The circumstances and costs associated with such a decision will clearly demand very careful consideration, negotiation and agreement. The exit strategy will need to address the potential security implications as well as the fiscal and contractual implications.

A decision to terminate a contract, especially as a result of a perceived breach of contract by the outsourcer, should not be made lightly. In addition to the legal risks associated with such a claim, there are likely to be serious consequences for the quality of the services and business operations, including potential reputational damage, as well as implications for contractor's staff transferred from the customer organization, who might be protected by employment rights under legislation such as the Transfer of Undertakings (Protection of Employment) Regulations 2006.

Outsourcing partnerships are similar in many ways to a marriage: with a lengthy courtship, a long-term commitment, serious consequences for failure to make it work, and potentially long and messy divorce proceedings. In fact, when partnerships begin to fail, a business equivalent to marriage guidance can help. There are many experienced consultancies specializing in providing advice on how to rescue or at least significantly improve the performance of a struggling outsourced service contract.

Termination of the contract should be seen as the last resort rather than the preferred solution. An exit strategy should consider the nature of the risks, as well as the associated business impacts from a major change in service provision. Such a strategy is an essential requirement of business continuity management. It is important also to plan for what happens after the relationship has ended. In particular, the customer must ensure that it is able either to contract with another competing third party provider, or to bring the services back in-house.

Outsourcing transfers a large amount of knowledge and control of business processes and information systems to the vendor. In fact, it might not be possible to move away from a supplier without their cooperation and continued support. Recognizing this dependence is not easy for an organization that has progressively lost visibility of day-to-day operations as a direct result of outsourcing.

Maintaining a basic understanding of the essential requirements for establishing an alternative source of services is vital to avoid excessive dependence on the existing supplier, and to ensure business continuity in the event of a major failure in service provision. It is, however, rarely practised to the extent necessary to escape dependence on the existing contractor. Like it or not, a swift exit from a major outsourcing deal is neither desirable nor possible without the support of the incumbent service provider. The absence of a realistic exit strategy implies a permanent dependency on the supplier.

Key questions to ask when considering review, termination and exit include the following.

- Is the end goal a conscious decision to exit the outsourcing arrangement, or simply the end of its natural life?
- How likely is an orderly transition of services, in each possible exit scenario?
- Are there significant risks of disruption which could have a serious business and security impact?
- Will the relationship turn bad when the arrangement comes to an end?
- Will the contract provide effective recourse for a major breakdown in relationship?

10.2 Exit and termination strategies

Development and maintenance of exit strategies should be closely coordinated with business continuity planning processes, as both address the requirements for contingency planning and fallback arrangements. In particular, it's important to maintain an up-to-date understanding of the key requirements for establishing an alternative service, in terms of software, data, documentation and other essential criteria such as minimum security, compliance and audit requirements.

Exit strategies should consider all of the options available, evaluate their potential implications, and design appropriate strategies to cover the following scenarios for termination of the contract:

- normal termination of the outsourcing agreement on expiration of the contract;
- termination for failure: an early exit from the arrangement as a result of failures that cannot be adequately resolved within the required timeframe;

- termination for convenience: the cancellation of the outsourcing agreement at will by either of the contracting parties;
- termination for regulatory requirements: cancellation or modification of an outsourcing agreement if required as a result of a major change in regulatory requirements.

Termination rights are vital to ensure that the customer can exercise the exit strategy. Even if the customer has no intention of exercising the termination rights, the mere fact that the option is available can help to improve the bargaining position for a better service or more attractive terms. In fact, the failure rate for outsourcing partnerships is surprisingly high: more than half of such partnerships are likely to fail within the first five years.

It should be noted that exit strategy planning is different from business continuity planning, as the latter essentially addresses many unexpected events and failures, but rarely considers unexpected termination, for example arising from a financial failure of the supplier. Exit strategy planning deals with scenarios that are anticipated, often with a degree of advanced warning, and in some cases as a desired outcome. The end result is also different, in that it is often likely that the status quo ante will not be restored.

If a party decides to exercise its right to terminate an outsourcing agreement, the contract should indicate the steps and timescales involved in disengaging and discharging its obligations. This is normally expressed in an agreed exit plan, detailing each party's responsibilities in handing back the delivery of the outsourced services. Such a plan must also address the consequences for ownership of assets and intellectual property, and it must be kept up-to-date, through periodic reviews.

It's worth noting, however, that the longer the outsourcing relationship continues, the greater will be the dependence on the outsourcer and the harder it will become to switch suppliers. Relationship management problems will also tend to grow, rather than diminish over time, unless immediately addressed. The most dangerous attitude, however, is simply to hope or assume that a difficult relationship will somehow get better. It certainly won't unless tackled head-on. Foresight and prompt action in responding to warning signals are crucial, especially as the rights of the customer and the obligations of the supplier can change significantly in the event of a failure, such as the bankruptcy of the outsourcer. Contractual conditions can help to limit exposure, but they will not deliver a fit-for-purpose service to business users.

Most important, from a security point of view, is that any termination arrangement should not result in a serious loss of security or business continuity arrangements, at least until the agreed termination date. There should be sufficient time available to enable the customer to arrange an alternative source of services.

The termination arrangements should also ensure that the costs involved and any obligations to employees affected, such as staff transferred to the contractor, are appropriately apportioned. The exit strategy will also need to address the requirements for the transition period to an alternative source of supply, including, for example, a suitable period of parallel running, and ensuring a minimum level of quality for the services delivered, as well as the need to ensure an appropriate level of skills and experience in the personnel delivering the service.

Consideration should be given also to the potential need to recruit experienced staff from the contractor, or to train up new staff in the operation of any transferred services, as well as the need to ensure the availability of essential supporting information such as inventories of assets and documentation such as system and platform configurations and detailed operating procedures.

A further important requirement of any exit process is to aim to maintain the relationship on the best possible terms. It is essential to ensure that, regardless of the loss of business, the supplier will continue to be motivated to deliver a professional service, up to and beyond the handover date.

10.3 Information security considerations

Information security considerations are especially important during the termination process. Key risks to address include

- the possibility of corruption, theft, loss or destruction of data transferred from the incumbent supplier to the new contractor, including live data, backups and archives,
- loss or theft of customer-owned hardware and software in the custody of the incumbent, including the risk of contravening terms of third-party software licences,
- risks to the confidentiality, integrity and availability of data and intellectual property, and

- the possibility of disaffected staff committing deliberate acts of theft, vandalism or disruption, arising, for example, from grievances relating to loss or transfer of employment rights and benefits.

A confidentiality agreement might be necessary, not just covering the information held by the contractor, but also regarding the decision to terminate the agreement, which might result in negative publicity and a loss in shareholder value if disclosed without consideration of the impact on public relations.

It will also be essential to make provision for the immediate return, or assured destruction, of all information that belongs to the organization, or which might compromise the security of its business processes or information systems. Consideration should also be given to the ownership and rights associated with third-party software licences and other valuable assets, including intellectual property generated by the partnership, as well as the need to comply with import or export regulations.

ISO/IEC 27036, an emerging International Standard for managing security in outsourcing, recommends that the customer organization should ensure that the outsourcer is required by contract to

- continue operating the outsourced service at the same level of quality during the transition period to a new service provider, and fully comply with the requirements specified in the outsourcing agreement,
- return all requested documentation at regular intervals during the transition period,
- provide access to its functions and resources supporting the outsourced service, if needed, to audit and identify any potential security weaknesses,
- provide parallel services for a certain period, with the right to extend the terms as necessary to resolve issues before the final cutover, and
- guarantee the confidentiality of any communications regarding the termination of the relationship.

In addition, the customer organization will need to

- specify responsibilities for the contracting or agreeing parties through and after the transition period,
- define the exit strategy team and its roles, including identifying any situations that should be evaluated,
- determine the roles and responsibilities when performing the final transfer of information and ICT resources,

- ensure the immediate transfer of all data belonging to it,
- keep the same personnel assigned on the outsourced service for the transition period,
- include the right to hire the personnel assigned by the supplier on the outsourced service in certain circumstances (e.g. termination for failure, bankruptcy),
- determine how the supplier shall destroy and remove the acquirer's information from all media, ensuring it is not disclosed to other individuals or organizations,
- recover or suspend any sub-licences transmitted to the supplier,
- specify the ICT resources and intellectual property provided to the supplier,
- require the supplier to provide access to ICT resources supporting the outsourced service, and
- ensure that the supplier fully documents any additional services during the transition period (e.g. training, configuration of ICT resources).

Agreement will be needed on compensation fees associated with the termination, including the costs of transition activities and any continuing services. The compensation arrangement for the transition period should be structured in a way to ensure that the supplier is motivated to perform its activities professionally through to their termination. At the completion of the outsourcing agreement, the customer organization should also ensure that

- the transition arrangement ends as specified in the exit strategy,
- all information, documentation and resources relating to the delivery of the outsourced services have been securely destroyed or transferred to the client, in accordance with the outsourcing agreement,
- an assurance and supporting evidence (reports, audit logs and signatures) are provided that the above information has been destroyed or returned, and
- all user accounts and related access rights granted to the outsourcer's personnel are withdrawn.

Exit strategies should be reviewed at regular intervals throughout the lifetime of the contract in order to ensure that the plans and arrangements remain both valid and optimal. Key changes to consider might include factors such as the following:

- the emergence of a new, alternative service that is substantially better, cheaper or more reliable than the services delivered by the outsourcer;
- the launch of a new technology or business application that is more attractive than the current offering from the outsourcer;

- trends in market pricing of services that might render the current arrangements uncompetitive;
- new regulatory compliance requirements that make significant demands on the outsourcer;
- changes in economic factors, such as interest rate fluctuations, which alter the nature of the underpinning business case for outsourcing;
- a proposal by the supplier to move elements of the service provision to offshore facilities, introducing new security and compliance issues that cannot be easily overcome.

Planning for the end of a contract might seem a low priority at the initial implementation stage, but in fact that is the very best time, when both the specification of services and the contract itself is fresh in the corporate memory, and the knowledge and experience of negotiating it is available to enable the customer to establish the rationale, key requirements and strategic options for a feasible exit strategy.

Managing the exit strategy is harder than it might at first appear. In particular, removing all traces of sensitive client information from the systems and premises of the outsourcer is far from easy. Customer data can find its way onto many shared devices, including back-up volumes and fallback systems. It is unrealistic to expect that such data would be encrypted or physically secured at all times in storage and transit. In practice this is unlikely. Many items of vital or sensitive information are easily overlooked. Examples of that might include systems documentation and encryption key material.

All information should be returned or securely destroyed with appropriate evidence of the fact, such as signed, witnessed certificates, immediately on the termination of the contract. In practice there will always be a degree of residual risk, as a complete erasure of every single trace of information and knowledge passed to the contractor will never be possible. Data will always be at risk of duplication without the customer's permission or knowledge.

Shared, distributed processing facilities, such as cloud computing services, present particular difficulty in ensuring that all customer data has been fully erased. Ideally they require the digital equivalent of a 'crumb detector' or 'data Hoover'. Many items of customer data, however, will continue to remain with the contractor. As with all aspects of outsourcing, we have no option but to accept a high degree of trust in the outsourcer. As my friend and colleague Philip Virgo once put it to me, 'We cannot empty the brains of the contractors.'

10.4 Learning points from this chapter

This chapter has explored the planning considerations and issues concerned with the eventual termination of the contract. Key learning points to note from can be summarized as follows.

▶ Outsourcing arrangements require extensive planning. Switching external service providers can take a long time. Planning for such changes needs to commence well in advance of any transfer. Contingency plans are also needed for unexpected failures or disputes that might result in a loss of services.

▶ The need for major changes can also prompt a rethink of sourcing arrangements. Mechanisms will be needed to anticipate significant changes in business needs, technology or market pricing. The contract should include arrangements for managing change, ranging from routine adjustments to a termination of contract.

▶ An agreed exit strategy should be established, supported by agreements that enable either party to terminate the contract prior to the end date. The absence of an exit strategy will result in a continued dependency on the supplier. The strategy should address security considerations, as well as financial and contractual implications. The steps and timescales involved will need to be expressed in an agreed exit plan.

▶ Exit strategies should cover all possible scenarios for termination, whether because of failure, convenience, contract expiration or changes in regulatory requirements. Termination rights are vital to ensure that the customer can exercise the exit strategy, as well as to improve the customer's bargaining position for a better service or more attractive terms. Exit strategies should be regularly reviewed to ensure that the plans remain valid and optimal.

▶ A decision to terminate a contract should not be made lightly, as there might be legal and reputational risks, as well as consequences for service quality, and for any staff transferred from the customer organization. It should be the last resort rather than the preferred solution.

▶ Outsourcing transfers a large amount of knowledge and control of business systems to the vendor. The longer the outsourcing relationship continues, the greater will be the dependence on the outsourcer and the harder it will be to switch suppliers. The relationship should be maintained on the best possible terms to ensure that the supplier is motivated to cooperate with the transfer and deliver a good service up to and beyond the handover date.

▶ It might be necessary to recruit experienced staff from the contractor, or to train up new staff in the operation of any transferred services. Access will also be needed to supporting information such as inventories of assets, system configurations and operating procedures.

▶ Exit strategies should be coordinated with business continuity planning, but they are different as they deal with anticipated scenarios with a degree of advance warning, and with an identified, desired outcome which is very different from the starting position.

▶ Security considerations are especially important during the termination process. Risks might include corruption of data, loss of assets, or perhaps deliberate acts of theft, vandalism or disruption. Arrangements must also be made for the immediate return or assured destruction of all customer information, including documentation and encryption keys, and for the withdrawal of all user accounts and access rights granted to the outsourcer's personnel.

▶ Removing all traces of sensitive client information from the systems and premises of the outsourcer is far from easy. Many items are easily overlooked. Data might be held on many shared devices, including back-up volumes and fallback systems. Knowledge will also remain indefinitely with the contractor's staff.

11 Security and risk in cloud computing

11.1 Cloud computing services

Cloud computing is a relatively new approach to IT service delivery that exploits the power of high-speed networks, virtualization technology and pervasive processing capability to deliver low-cost, highly scalable computing services. The economic potential of cloud computing can be illustrated by a surprising statistic that indicates that most computer servers run at 15% or less of their capability.[8] And even if you could manage to utilize as much as 70% of your available in-house capacity, it's possible that you could achieve at least a short-term saving by moving to an external cloud computing supplier.

There is, therefore, huge potential for step changes in efficiency and costs from exploiting techniques and technology that enable greater sharing of hardware resources. The use of services delivered from within a network cloud, however, implies that the user does not know, or even care, where the data actually resides, or how it is stored and processed. That concept in itself presents a challenge for security. Such a degree of uncertainty is anathema to security managers, who generally rely on good visibility of risks and events, and a capability to intervene quickly in order to mitigate risks.

Speed and ease of implementation is also a major feature of cloud services. A business manager armed with a credit card can purchase and implement a cloud computing service within minutes, bypassing many procurement and security checks, which assume that IT services are provided through a controlled purchasing process.

Throughout this book, the importance has been emphasized of carefully specifying security requirements, negotiating contractual conditions and carrying out a thorough examination of the outsourcer's security capability. The whole point of a cloud computing service, however, is to achieve business benefits through sharing of common services and massive economies of scale. Most cloud services are generally intended to be low-cost, standardized

---

[8] Reported by TreeHugger, an environmental media company in 2008.

products by nature, not ones that are designed to accommodate extensive tailoring and auditing by individual customers.

This scenario can present a major challenge for due diligence and contract negotiation. Excessive customer intrusions or personalization demands can undermine the fundamental economics of cloud computing. On the other hand, unquestioned acceptance of a cloud service provider's conditions and security posture is certainly not a sensible move from a risk-management perspective.

The ideal solution is, in fact, for cloud service providers to deliver a high level of continuous security assurance that is sufficient to meet or exceed the security requirements of the vast majority of users, with enough independent evidence supplied to satisfy the most demanding of security managers and auditors. This justifies the development of a new, higher security standard for large cloud service operators, and a strict standard for the professional skills and capabilities of the auditors delivering the independent assurance that is required.

When it comes to considering the security risks and requirements associated with cloud computing, it is important to appreciate that there is no standard model that can be used. Cloud services are offered at various levels of abstraction, ranging from the provision of basic infrastructure right through to the delivery of high-level business applications. There are many different usage models and options, and the risks, costs and the necessary governance processes will vary greatly between different implementations, generally becoming richer and more specific the higher in the value chain that the service is delivered.

11.2 Forms of cloud computing services

Cloud computing is a term that covers several different concepts. There is no single model for delivering a cloud computing service. Each service offers a particular blend of service and functionality, ranging from the simple delivery of raw processing power at the platform level, to the delivery of sophisticated higher-level business services. Cloud computing services offer varying degrees of cost savings, functionality, flexibility, sharing and availability, each combination presenting a different set of security risks.

An important feature of cloud computing services is the concept of abstraction of detail between layers. Cloud models aim to provide a degree of separation

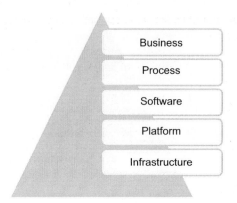

Figure 8 – Layers of cloud services

between layers of service delivery, isolating processes from software, and platforms from infrastructure. In theory this provides assurance that the use of cloud services at one layer will not impact the management and security controls operating at other levels in the infrastructure. But, in practice, cloud services can open up new areas of risk, as well as opportunities for security improvements, at all levels of management control.

11.3 A hierarchy of services

The various categories of cloud services can be thought of as a hierarchical set of products, enabling a customer to build a complete set of business services from a portfolio of underpinning outsourced services, ranging from the acquisition of raw processing power to the delivery of sophisticated business services, as illustrated in Figure 8.

Most cloud computing services fall into one of the three lower categories, termed Software-as-a-Service, Platform-as-a-Service and Infrastructure-as-a-Service. Each of these layers presents a slightly different set of challenges, risks and benefits.

The solution space and services on offer, however, is rapidly evolving and continuously maturing. In particular, many services are becoming richer and more configurable, and risks and controls are becoming increasingly apparent[9] and subsequently being addressed. Over the next decade we are also likely to see the emergence of increasingly sophisticated cloud services that can function as a complete business process or even an entire line of business.

Software-as-a-Service

Software-as-a-Service is a model of software provision that enables business applications or utilities to be delivered on demand through a public network. Such services have continued to grow in both popularity and maturity since the beginning of the century, when they were first pioneered by innovative vendors such as salesforce.com. Service providers generally host their business applications through a private Web server connected to the Internet. Alternatively, they might provide software that can be downloaded across the Internet to a consumer device.

Platform-as-a-Service

Platform-as-a-Service enables business applications to be developed and run on top of a specific execution platform that is hosted in the cloud. This option requires careful scrutiny to ensure that the configuration of the platform is sufficiently secure, as well as close attention to technical architecture in order to minimize the effort and the risks associated with both the short-term migration and the longer-term maintenance of business applications. Shared platforms also introduce the potential risk that a rogue customer might install malicious software that creates damaging side effects for other users sharing that platform.

Infrastructure-as-a-Service

Infrastructure-as-a-Service is a less ambitious approach which retains the existing business applications, running on a virtual machine image provided by the service provider. It avoids many migration issues and presents a much lower risk of longer-term vendor lock-in. The business benefits are limited, however, compared to other forms of cloud services. Generally, the lower layers of the cloud computing model allow a much greater degree of tailoring of information

---

[9] At the beginning of 2009 there was not a single published guide to the security of cloud computing. By the end of 2009 several had been published, though many aspects of the problem space still remain to be addressed.

systems. This flexibility helps to reduce dependence on particular vendors, but at the same time it can limit the potential to exploit the higher levels in the model.

11.4 The importance of architecture

Cloud computing architectures can have a major impact on the functionality and security of business applications. Cloud service providers, for example, are more inclined to exploit lower levels of cloud services delivered by other vendors. Use of a stack of cloud services will further restrict the scope for tailored security configurations. It will also extend the scope of due diligence, and complicate attempts to assess the potential impact of new security threats or major service changes.

From a functionality perspective, however, these service models will also be much more accessible to users and business partners, enabling the rapid establishment of temporary facilities, sharing of collaborative applications, or the use of highly scalable specialist services from any global location or client device. These models are therefore highly attractive to customer organizations that wish to move to a variable-cost model, perhaps in anticipation of a future reduction in service demand, or to those that intend to implement collaborative business processes with a range of external organizations, or who simply need large amounts of temporary computing power on an ad hoc basis.

11.5 Benefits and risks

Cloud services are much faster to deploy and offer quicker incorporation of new features, patches or upgrades to new releases of software. They need not be less secure than equivalent in-house services, as they can offer more up-to-date security features and afford to employ professional security management. But the use of cloud services will inevitably introduce new sources of business and security risk, through the loss of visibility and direct control over the management of services.

Cloud applications are also likely to offer many proprietary features to entice new customers. The risk is that it might not be possible to replicate these features through alternatively sourced services, creating a high dependency on a single vendor. Such a dependency can potentially restrict future strategy, as well as present a challenge for business continuity planning.

11.6 Security services in the cloud

Cloud services are also becoming an increasingly popular mechanism for delivering information security services, such as vulnerability scanning of networked computer platforms to detect security weaknesses, or filtering and scanning Internet content to detect malware or instances of inappropriate access.

The concept of a security service being accessed through the Internet might raise a few eyebrows, but such services can offer substantial benefits over an in-house alternative, as they have a much broader perspective on security risks through the continuous monitoring of events across a large community of users, rather than just within an individual enterprise.

The fact that many Fortune 100 companies have already deployed a range of cloud-based services for both business and security applications demonstrates that the security risks associated with such services can be mitigated to an acceptable level, at least in selected deployments. Any use of unknown third party security services, however, will inevitably present a major security exposure, so special care should be taken in evaluating the capabilities, motivation and track record of the companies delivering such services.

11.7 Security opportunities presented by cloud technologies

The virtualization technologies that underpin cloud computing also offer potential for new security solutions, although these are some years away from being deployed in mainstream business applications. The use of such technology can, for example, enable multiple clients or identities to share a single platform or device with less risk of a compromise caused by one client infecting other users of that device.[10] A further potential technique is to divide a physical server into several virtual servers that are rotated and refreshed each second, reducing the risk of a vulnerability being exploited by an attacker who might have gained access.[11]

---

[10] Secure architectures based on this concept are being developed by leading vendors such as HP.
[11] George Mason University has developed a security solution based on this concept.

11.8 Models for cloud computing usage

Leading authorities differ slightly on how to categorize cloud computing models, but are generally united on the general principles and problems associated with them. The US National Institute of Standards and Technology has defined five essential characteristics, three service models and four deployment models. Gartner, a leading IT analyst, has proposed six different models. And the Jericho Forum, an international thought leadership security circle, suggests that there are as many as 40 different combinations of cloud service provision and use models. But the key useful points to establish are the commonalities and differences in security risks, requirements and architecture between the various flavours of cloud computing models.

Cloud services can be private (owned or leased), shared, public, or constructed from a hybrid mixture of some or all of these options. The Jericho Forum and the Cloud Computing Alliance, two leading private groups formed of both user organizations and computer vendors, have been studying the business operating models and security implications associated with cloud computing. Among other conclusions, they have identified four distinct criteria to differentiate the various forms of cloud computing from a security perspective.

These are partially illustrated in Figure 9, which illustrates three of the criteria. The fourth criterion (in-sourced or outsourced) unfortunately does not fit on a three-dimensional drawing.

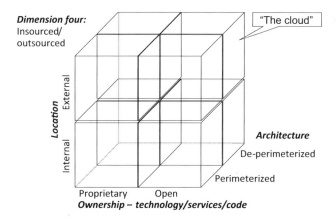

Figure 9 – Jericho Forum illustration of cloud service models

Internal or external cloud services

The first criterion is whether the physical location of the data is inside or outside of the user organization's controlled boundaries. An example of an internal cloud service might be the use of virtualized hard disks within the organization's data centre. At first sight this might seem irrelevant to a discussion on outsourcing, but it's important to consider the contrast in risks, especially as many implementations will tend to combine both internal and external options.

An example of an external cloud service would be the use of third-party storage services delivered from an off-site location. Each of these options presents a different set of benefits and risks. The use of in-house storage enables greater control over the processing environment, but an external service might offer a better set of security features to support external collaborative working, for example, or to ensure disaster recovery.

From a security management perspective, the main differences between the two options concern the governance and compliance arrangements, which will need to be extended and at least partially executed by third-party staff operating outside the corporate boundary. This can be further complicated by the implementations that exploit a combination of both internal and external sourcing, requiring a versatile approach to both policy and auditing.

Proprietary or open cloud services

The second criterion is whether the service is based on proprietary or open standards. By that we mean whether the technology, services and interfaces are controlled exclusively by the supplier, or whether they are based on openly available technology standards. Again, each of these approaches presents a different set of benefits and business risks.

Open standards enable a higher degree of interoperability and transportability of data and applications between systems and services, including the ability to interface with other forms of hosted service and to change service providers with relative ease. In contrast, proprietary cloud services might introduce restrictions on sharing and transportation of applications, though they are likely to offer unique, innovative features protected through patents or trade secrets.

Clearly, each approach presents a different set of commercial business risks. But there are also likely to be significant differences in the range of security features provided with each service, as well as in their capability to incorporate countermeasures from third-party sources. For many organizations, a further major security consideration will be the ease with which data can be shared with outside parties, as well as the mechanisms available to help secure such collaborations.

Protected or de-perimeterized cloud applications

The third criterion represents the architectural assumptions behind the hosting environment and, in particular, whether the organization's information systems and supporting infrastructure were designed to operate within a protected corporate IT perimeter, or whether a 'de-perimeterized' philosophy has been adopted to enable them to operate securely across a range of network environments of varying degrees of trustworthiness, including within public networks such the Internet.

In the former case, any systems and data that need to be shared across organizational boundaries will have to be safeguarded through an extension of the corporate network environment by, for example, creating a virtual private network for the duration of the external access session.

Central to the consideration of this criterion is the question of *context*, i.e. whether the systems, data and services can be securely operated within a different environment from the one for which they were originally designed. Cloud computing presents a very different security context, demanding, in many cases, much stronger mechanisms for authentication, encryption and vulnerability management.

In-sourced or outsourced cloud services

The fourth criterion is whether the responsibility for delivering the cloud service is in-sourced or outsourced. For the purposes of this book, we will concentrate on the outsourced option, which presents the major challenge of due diligence, i.e. the need to validate the trustworthiness of the third party as well as the security capability of the service offered.

This is a challenging task, as cloud computing is a relatively new form of service offering for which we have yet to establish mature security standards and comprehensive audit checklists. The task is further complicated by the likelihood that the service might be delivered from multiple, remote locations, and the service provider might not be prepared to cooperate with audits or inspections.

Developing an in-house cloud computing service might, at first sight, appear to be a sensible first step towards realizing the benefits of this new form of service delivery. In practice, however, it is unlikely to offer the same features and economies of scale as an external service, and such a compromise can introduce an additional set of complex changes on the longer-term journey to a fully externalized service.

But regardless of the path chosen for the journey from in-house to external computing services, it is likely that, in most cases, enterprises will need to operate a combination of internal and external infrastructure, with complex interfaces and a need to govern and audit systems and services whose custodianship extends across corporate boundaries.

11.9 Risks associated with cloud computing

For many organizations, cloud computing introduces a radical shift in thinking about the very nature of governance processes, demanding an acceptance of the concept that custodianship of sensitive data and services can be safely delegated to a remote third party operating an external, invisible infrastructure shared by many other customers.

From one perspective, we can compare it with the use of everyday electronic banking and e-commerce services, which most of us are comfortable in using without any hesitation. But there are key differences between the occasional use of systems designed specifically for e-commerce, and the transfer of critical legacy business systems to a less secure operating environment.

It is also important to recognize that not every third-party service provider is capable of delivering an equal level of security protection, so this degree of uncertainty needs to be carefully calculated and managed. In particular, questions will need to be asked about the degree of segregation of stored and processed data from other users of the cloud service, as well as the level of access granted to service managers, and the range of checks and controls applied to protect against internal and external breaches or misuse of sensitive data.

The implications for regulatory compliance must also be addressed, as the supplier's standard terms and conditions might not be sufficient to meet specific legal, compliance or audit requirements. Indeed, some cloud services are not suitable for processing credit card transactions, for example, because the service providers are not able to provide either the access or guarantee of compliance required to meet the Payment Card Industry Data Security Standard.

If the data that will be stored and processed in the cloud service includes personal data on customers or employees then there will be obligations under European data protection rules for the data controller (the customer organization) to ensure that appropriate security measures are put in place to safeguard the data. This is complicated by the fact that the level of security that might be deemed appropriate is not absolute, but depends on the sensitivity of the data and the harm that might arise from a data breach. Establishing this will require a risk assessment to be carried out, a review of the security controls applied by the service provider, a contract that specifies an appropriate level of security, and suitable processes to monitor and maintain this level of protection.

Data protection requirements can also be impacted by a transfer to a different jurisdiction. In particular, there are restrictions on transfers of personal data outside of Europe unless an adequate level of protection can be ensured. If the data centre is in the USA, this can be achieved by the service provider adhering to the 'safe harbour' framework developed by the US Department of Commerce and the European Commission. Personal data can also be sent outside of the European Union if a model contract is put in place.

These methods, however, do not allow any sharing of the data with subcontractors, which can present problems for many cloud service operators. The current regulatory trend towards mandatory reporting of any data breaches affecting individuals will also require close cooperation with the service provider, to ensure that such breaches can be promptly identified, reported, investigated and remedied.

In addition, the fact that data will be spread across a shared infrastructure encompassing a range of legal jurisdictions introduces a range of new risks, ranging from issues raised by legal discovery demands to those presented by confiscations of computer servers as evidence by law enforcement investigators.

As with all outsourcing arrangements, cloud computing demands careful attention to the contractual conditions to avoid subsequent legal issues, including even the possibility that the supplier might claim rights to the use or ownership of data or intellectual property stored in the cloud. For many low-cost, commodity cloud services such contracts might not be negotiable, presenting significant residual risks and liabilities.

A further consideration is the impact of a transfer to a cloud service on existing arrangements for information sharing or collaboration with third parties, which can reduce or heighten certain security risks. In-house services enable tighter control of third-party access to data, but they can also present a risk to other enterprise systems and infrastructure through the need to open up the network perimeter to external business partners. Organizations might view the move to a cloud computing model as a convenient solution to existing infrastructure management problems. But in practice this is unlikely to be the case, as system migration issues and the need for new skills are likely to present many demanding short-term and long-term challenges.

The move to cloud computing presents no less than a radical shift in IT planning, architecture and operational management. Service levels associated with cloud computing services might be less guaranteed than the same levels that can be achieved within a private, dedicated network. Cloud services, as well as the public networks they rely on, are designed to be readily scalable, but they are also intended to be operated at a much higher level of utilization, presenting a potentially higher risk during periods of peak activity and demand.

Moving from a devolved set of services to a large, centralized, standardized service can also present a greater risk from single-point failures, for example a security flaw or catastrophic failure in the hypervisor software that manages the underpinning virtualization process, which would result in large-scale disruption of services. Areas such as network performance management, business continuity management and the ability to prioritize business applications will become increasingly critical to ensuring the quality and continued delivery of critical business services.

Transactions within a cloud application service are unlikely to be encrypted to protect them from unauthorized viewing or interception, but the same restriction generally applies to most in-house services. What is different is that any decision to incorporate such a safeguard will be largely in the hands of the cloud service provider, who will need to cooperate with such a change, as well as being technically and operationally capable of applying such countermeasures.

11.10 Learning points from this chapter

This chapter has explored the security issues associated with cloud computing services. Key learning points to note can be summarized as follows.

▶ Cloud computing is a new approach to IT service delivery, offering greater efficiency and lower costs through sharing of hardware and software resources. The user might have no assurances as to where the data resides, or how it is stored and processed, presenting a new set of challenges for security managers.

▶ In previous chapters we have emphasized the need for detailed specifications of security requirements, carefully negotiated contracts, and thorough examination of the outsourcer's capabilities. This does not fit the world of cloud computing, which aims to deliver cheap, generic services through economies of scale.

▶ Cloud services are not usually designed to accommodate tailoring and auditing by individual customers, presenting constraints for due diligence and contract negotiation. The ideal solution is for the cloud service providers to provide ongoing, independent security assurances for users and their auditors. This justifies the development of a new security standard, as well as a strict standard for the professional skills and capabilities of the auditors.

▶ Cloud services need not be less secure than in-house services, as they can offer more up-to-date security features and employ professional security management. But an additional degree of risk will inevitably be introduced through loss of visibility and direct control over the management of services.

▶ Cloud services can be private, shared or public. They can operate at the application or infrastructure level. Systems can be protected through private infrastructure or made secure to operate across public networks. Most enterprises will need a combination of these options, resulting in complex interfaces and governance processes.

▶ Different cloud service providers can provide varying levels of security protection. Questions should be asked about the degree of segregation of data from other users of the cloud service, as well as the level of access granted to service managers, and the range of checks and controls to safeguard against breaches or misuse of data.

▶ Large, centralized, standardized services can also present risks from single-point failures, for example a flaw or catastrophic failure of the hypervisor software that manages virtualization process or the external networks that connect users. Cloud applications offer many proprietary features to entice new customers, which can present a challenge for fallback and business continuity planning.

▶ Cloud services can also deliver information security services which offer benefits over in-house services, through their broader perspective on threats and incidents across a larger community of users. Care should be taken in evaluating the capabilities and motivation of vendors offering such services.

▶ The supplier's standard terms and conditions might not be sufficient to meet legal, compliance or audit requirements. Payment card data will need to be protected to the Payment Card Industry Data Security Standard. Personal data on customers or employees will need to be safeguarded in accordance with data protection legislation, which can restrict transfers to different jurisdictions. Careful attention is required to contractual conditions, including the possibility that the supplier might claim rights to the use or ownership of data or intellectual property stored in the cloud.

As a final note, I am reminded of Dr Alastair MacWillson's warning in his foreword to this book: 'Organizations must be vigilant when it comes to confirming the security posture of the companies with which they do business, especially as business takes them to countries with differing standards for data protection and privacy. Always remember the maxim: *choose your business partners with care!'*

Bibliography

Allery, Philip: *Tolley's effective Outsourcing: Practice and Procedure*, Tottel Publishing, 2004.

Benn, Ian & Jill Pearcy: *Strategic Outsourcing: Exploiting the Skills of Third Parties*, Hodder & Stoughton, 2003.

Bravard, Jean-Louis & Robert Morgan: *Smarter Outsourcing: An executive guide to understanding, planning and exploiting successful outsourcing relationships*, Prentice Hall, 2009.

Brudenall, Peter (Editor): *Technology and Offshore Outsourcing Strategies*, Palgrave Macmillan, 2005.

Davies, Paul: *What's this India Business? Offshoring, Outsourcing, and the Global Services Revolution*, Nicholas Brealey Publishing, 2004.

Fisher, Roger & William Ury: *Getting to YES: Negotiating Agreement Without Giving In*, Penguin, 1991.

Heywood, J Brian: *The Outsourcing Dilemma – The Search for Competitiveness*, Prentice Hall-Gale, 2001.

Hofstede, Geert & Gert-Jan Hofstede: *Cultures and Organizations – Software of the Mind* (2nd ed), McGraw-Hill, 2005.

Jenster, Per V & Henrik Stener Pedrersen, Patricia Plackett, David Hussey: *Outsourcing Insourcing*, The Chartered Institute of Purchasing & Supply, 2005.

Kakabadse, Andrew & Nada Kakabadse: *Smart Sourcing – International Best Practice*, Palgrave MacMillan, 2002.

Kobayashi-Hillary, Mark: *Outsourcing to India – The Offshore Advantage* (2nd ed), Springer, 2005.

Lacey, David: *Managing the Human Factor in Information Security: How to Win Over Staff and Influence Business Managers*, John Wiley, 2009.

Lewis, Amanda: *Outsourcing Contracts – A Practical Guide*, City & Financial Publishing, 2005.

Bibliography

McIvor, Ronan: *The Outsourcing Process – Strategies for Evaluation and Management*, Cambridge University Press, 2005.

Nierenberg, Gerard: *The Art of Negotiating*, Barnes Noble, 1968.

NISCC Good Practice Guide, *Outsourcing: Security Governance Framework for IT Managed Service Provision*, National Infrastructure Security Coordination Centre, 2006 (available at www.cpni.gov.uk).

Patel, Alpesh B: *Outsourcing Success – The Management Imperative*, Palgrave MacMillan, 2005.

Pepper, Bill & Bridget: *Intellect Data Security and Data Protection Guidelines for Offshoring and Outsourcing*, Intellect 2008 (published to members only at www.intellectuk.org).

Power, Mark J & Kevin Desouza, Carlo Bonifazi: *The Outsourcing Handbook – How to Implement a Successful Outsourcing Process*, Kogan Page, 2006.

Sajeev, ASM & Sakgasit Ramingwong: 'Mum Effect as an Offshore Outsourcing Risk: A Study of Differences in Perceptions', *Computer Journal*, (53:1), Oxford, 2010.

Sparrow, Elizabeth Anne: *A Guide to Global Sourcing – Offshore Outsourcing and Other Global Delivery Models*, The British Computer Society, 2004.

Standards

BS 7858, Security *screening of individuals employed in a security environment – Code of practice*.

BS 25999-1, *Business Continuity Management – Code of Practice*.

BS 25999-2, *Specification for business continuity management*.

BS EN ISO 9001, *Quality management systems – Requirements*.

BS EN ISO 14001, *Environmental management systems – Requirements with guidance for use*.

BS ISO 28000, *Specification for security management systems for the supply chain*.

BS ISO 28001, *Security management systems for the supply chain – Best practices for implementing supply chain security, assessments and plans – Requirements and guidance.*

BS ISO 28003, *Security management systems for the supply chain – Requirements for bodies providing audit and certification of supply chain security management systems.*

BS ISO 28004, *Security management systems for the supply chain – Guidelines for the implementation of ISO 28000.*

BS ISO 31000, *Risk management – Principles and guidelines.*

BS ISO/IEC 20000, *Information technology – Service management.*

BS ISO/IEC 27001, *Information technology – Security techniques – Information security management systems – Requirements.*

BS ISO/IEC 27002, *Information technology – Security techniques – Code of practice for information security management.*

BS ISO/IEC 27005, *Information technology – Security techniques – Information security risk management.*

Control Objectives for Information and related Technology (COBIT) Version 4.1, IT Governance Institute, 2007.

PAS 99, *Specification of common management system requirements as a framework for integration.*

Payment Card Industry (PCI) Data Security Standard, PCI Security Standard Council, 2009.

PD ISO/IEC Guide 73, *Risk management – Vocabulary – Guidelines for use in standards.*

Additional references

Statement on Auditing Standard No 70: Service Organizations, The American Institute of Certified Public Accountants, 1992.

The Information Technology Infrastructure Library (ITIL), TSO, 2007.

Index

Index

Index

If you found this book useful, you may also want to buy:

Information Security Risk Management: Handbook for ISO/IEC 27001
Edward Humphreys

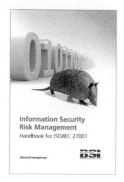

The focus of this book is based around the concept of having an information security management system (ISMS) as a framework for achieving the effective management of information security risks. International standard ISO/IEC 27001 is a world recognized standard for establishing, implementing, monitoring and reviewing, updating and improving an ISMS. ISO/IEC 27005 is an ISMS risk management standard that supports the implementation of ISO/IEC 27001.

This book is aimed at those business managers and staff involved in ISMS risk management activities. It is a practical handbook for the use and application of ISO/IEC 27005. It provides guidance and advice to specifically support the implementation of those requirements specified in ISO/IEC 27001:2005 that relate to risk management processes and associated activities.

- A5 paperback · ISBN 9780 580 60745 5 · 153pp · £38.95 · April 2010
- For more details see http://shop.bsigroup.com/bip0076

Cloud Computing: A Practical Introduction to the Legal Issues
Renzo Marchini

Much is being said about cloud computing, and in particular the benefits (both economic and environmental) and the risks. But how are those involved in buying IT to judge the legal issues which arise, and how can contracts maximize the advantages and minimize the disadvantages? How can cloud service providers address the customer's legal concerns so that the proposition remains viable for the customer and their own business?

This book will introduce cloud computing (briefly) for those new to the concept, comparing the development of this new computing paradigm to other ways of buying computing resource. It will summarize the legal issues which arise, some of which are unique to cloud, others of which are more general but have a unique application to cloud.

It will explore these legal issues, covering such areas as security in the cloud, data protection, service levels, and contractual issues. It will provide a practical resource for those involved in buying or providing cloud services, setting out practical steps to address legal issues both in the regulatory context and in the context of contracts between customer and suppliers. It also deals with issues which arise when the cloud service is used by regulated sectors, such as financial services.

- A5 paperback · ISBN 978 0 580 70322 5 · 200pp · £30.00 · November 2010
- For more details see http://shop.bsigroup.com/bip0117